Greening The City
A Guide to Good Practice

November 1996

A Report for the Department of the Environment

By GFA Consulting in association with Tibbalds Monro

ISBN 0 11 753335 1

Produced by DDP Services
B9258   October 1996
Printed in the United Kingdom on recycled paper

Contents

Greening the City: *Guide to Good Practice*

Foreword

by the Rt Hon John Gummer MP, Secretary of State for the Environment

The Greening the City initiative was launched in October 1995, and follows up a commitment in the Rural White Paper to develop national good practice for urban greening.

Over the last year, I have been impressed with the way in which "Greening the City" has captured the imagination of so many individuals and organisations, all willing to share their experience and expertise. The case studies contained within this guide provide excellent illustrations of what is being achieved, which I hope others will be encouraged to follow.

We all have a part to play in developing ways of improving and enhancing the appearance and use of our towns and cities, whether as policy makers, local authority decision-makers, developers or ordinary citizens. However, attention often tends to focus on buildings themselves, with relatively little concern for the spaces around and in between them. In future, we must look at development in a more comprehensive and coordinated way to ensure a better quality environment for everyone. The provision of good quality greening schemes in urban areas is central to the holistic approach.

Executive summary

Greening the City

The Greening the City initiative was launched by the Government in 1995 to promote discussion and ideas about the creation, protection, management and maintenance of green areas in our towns and cities; draw together examples of good practice; and encourage new ideas about, and approaches to, landscape design. This report and guide to good practice has been produced from the findings of six seminars and research into 22 good practice case studies.

Why Urban Greening?

This report explores the range of benefits that the appropriate greening of urban developments can provide, in addition to simply improving the appearance of sites. Most of these offer long term social, economic and environmental improvements. The key benefits are:

- helping inward investment and business retention by improving the image of an area;
- environmental benefits, including pollution control, enhancing biodiversity and contributing to sustainable development;
- enhanced quality of life for people living and working in the area;
- educational, social and cultural advantages, improving leisure and recreational facilities;
- providing a positive environmental image for businesses and encouraging tourism;
- contributing to healthier lifestyles and community development.

Urban greening is therefore not just a cosmetic afterthought: it is a key component of regeneration and can help to ensure developments are sustainable. Good practice requires a strategic approach in which greening principles are located at the heart of the planning process and regeneration strategies.

Case study findings

The report highlights good practice through 22 case studies drawn from all over England. Key areas which are discussed include:

- involving local communities: this constitutes a fundamental aspect of good practice in the design and implementation of greening initiatives, and should be embarked on as early as possible within the planning/development process. Involving local people is a key feature of all publicly funded regeneration activity, not only to ensure that the development is acceptable to local people and will be used, but also to encourage local ownership and pride as a means of securing continuing protection and maintenance.

- planning and design: greening is a long term activity – and this needs to be reflected in project planning and arrangements for funding. The key to effective project management is a comprehensive master plan – particularly for large and complex projects, with several partners, and multiple funding sources.

- funding: project managers need to develop the necessary skills to secure a suitable 'cocktail' of funds from a variety of sources such as the Government challenge fund, the private sector and the lottery. Local authorities can no longer be expected to fund environmental projects on their own. As pressure on their budgets increases, their mainstream responsibilities take priority. For greening schemes the question of long term revenue funding is especially acute. However, the Guide identifies a variety of greening initiatives, where contributions from private sector partners have helped provide support for long term management and maintenance; where there are opportunities for the commercial exploitation of greening initiatives; and where cost-effective planting and maintenance enable improvements to be achieved without additional resources.

- partnerships: partnership working arrangements which include local communities and the private sector alongside public agencies, are a fundamental part of effective greening. Productive partnerships require an organisation prepared to take the lead; a willingness by key agencies to share decision-making; clarity of purpose; and adequate support resources.

- management, maintenance and monitoring: greening initiatives require active management as well as maintenance. Proper management and monitoring of green space is important to ensure that projects have the capacity to adapt over time to changing participants and to new demands on the landscape and land use.

Recommendations

The report is designed to build on and extend existing good practice by:

- **encouraging** local authorities (together with their key partners) to adopt a strategic approach and incorporate greening at the heart of the statutory planning process;

- **persuading** developers, owners and occupiers of residential, industrial and commercial land of the economic, as well as the environmental advantages of adopting green design principles as an integral part of the development process;

- **inviting** the voluntary sector to become involved in the greening process, as partners in local projects, to develop their own skills in capacity building and to contribute local knowledge and views;

- **demonstrating** how greening initiatives can meet a wide range of objectives simultaneously – economic, environmental and social – through consultation, sensitive project design and local partnerships.

Acknowledgements

In undertaking this assignment we have received substantial and enthusiastic help from a wide variety of people and organisations, too numerous to mention individually. They include:

- all those who contributed to the seminar programme, as speakers and delegates;
- the many people who gave up time, to show us round and explain their projects;
- the members of the DOE's external advisory group whose experience and suggestions have contributed to our understanding of the issues;
- the officials in the Department who have steered the project with patience.

As always, responsibility for the report is ours; but it would not be what it is without this help.

Greening the City: *Guide to Good Practice*

1 Introduction

In 1995 the Government launched the Greening the City initiative to:

- promote discussion and ideas about the creation, protection, management, and maintenance of green areas in our towns and cities;

- draw together examples of good practice; and

- encourage new ideas about, and approaches to, landscape design.

GFA Consulting, together with Tibbalds Monro, was commissioned to undertake a programme of research to identify the lessons arising from current practice. The work included:

- a series of consultation seminars to draw on the views and experience of experts and practitioners in the field;

- interviews with representatives of key agencies with an interest in urban greening;

- reviewing the substantial literature of relevance to urban greening;

- a series of case studies, chosen to illuminate a variety of types of environmental initiative.

> *'A better environment in our towns and cities not only enhances the quality of life for those of us who live there but also helps to relieve pressure on the countryside... improving the urban environment is a pre-requisite for the proper protection of rural England.'*
>
> **Rural White Paper**
>
> **(HMSO, 1995)**

A theme which has dominated the study, and which is reflected in this guide, is the importance of adopting a strategic approach to the physical 'greening' of the urban environment, rather than relying simply on an incremental project-led approach. To explore how individual projects relate to their environmental, geographical and economic context, six of our case studies focused on the Black Country. The remainder are based on individual projects throughout the country, though we were enormously encouraged to discover that, in most cases, the projects were developed as part of a wider strategy.

The Greening the City initiative's immediate origins lie in the 1995 Rural White Paper, which saw the improvement of the urban environment as a prerequisite for protecting the countryside. But developing greener urban environments is a key component of 'sustainable development' (Figure 1). A commitment to more sustainable patterns of development (known as Agenda 21) by more than 150 states, including the UK, was one of the outcomes of the Earth Summit in Rio de Janeiro in 1992.

Figure 1: Sustainable urban development

Sustainable development has been defined as that which:

- '...meets the needs of the present without compromising the ability of future generations to meet their own needs.'

For towns and cities, elements of sustainable development include:

- compact settlements to allow lower energy consumption;

- local amenities to reduce the need for travel;

- improving the quality of urban life to reduce development pressure in the countryside;

- creating and protecting green space.

Source: Sustainable Development: The UK Strategy, (HMSO, 1994)

What do we mean by 'greening'?

In this guide we have adopted a broad interpretation of the notion of greening. It embraces the networks of green space which make up the urban landscape, including:

- green corridors that follow transportation networks;
- parks and gardens;
- river valleys within urban environments;
- natural wild spaces;
- urban forestry;
- community woodlands;
- street trees;
- community gardens and nature areas;
- cemeteries and allotments;
- playing fields and playgrounds;
- derelict and despoiled vacant land;
- land temporarily vacant awaiting development;
- planting in public spaces within town centres, industrial, commercial and residential areas;
- planting on buildings: ie green roofs.

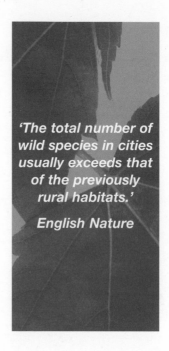

'The total number of wild species in cities usually exceeds that of the previously rural habitats.'

English Nature

Why is greening important?

In many of our older inner cities or industrial areas, the symptoms of environmental dereliction are highly visible – polluted waterways, contaminated land, redundant industrial buildings or drab and dilapidated housing estates. But the range of environmental problems facing urban areas is much wider. Figure 2 offers a summary from an OECD publication.

Figure 2: Environmental problems facing urban areas

- air pollution;
- water pollution;
- waste;
- noise generation;
- pressure on land for urban development;
- deterioration in quality of urban life;
- degradation of urban landscape.

Source: Environmental Policies for Cities in the 1990s, (OECD, 1990)

The problems are pressing and substantial, but in our response to them it is important to be sensitive to the strengths of our towns and cities, and to ensure that what is valuable is protected as the dereliction is removed. Many of our case studies show sensitivity to ecology and habitat, and a recognition that cities already provide rich and plentiful resources for a wide variety of plants and animals, some of which feature in UK programmes supporting the conservation of global biodiversity. Strategies for urban greening must reflect the issues surrounding sustainability and the principles of nature conservation – and protecting those species which have already successfully colonised urban areas – as well as promoting diversification.

The purpose of this Guide

This Guide is designed to offer advice on good practice in the development of strategies for urban greening, as well as the design, implementation and management of greening projects. It is one of a series of complementary guides recently published by the Department of the Environment, including:

- Vital and Viable Town Centres: Meeting The Challenge (HMSO, 1994);
- The Impact of Environmental Improvements in Urban Regeneration (HMSO, 1995);
- People, Parks and Cities: A Guide to Current Good Practice in Urban Parks (HMSO, 1996).

The case studies offer a picture of what is being done, while in the main section, we explore how, and develop key principles. The guide is aimed at policy makers, and those with an interest in environmental initiatives, from a variety of perspectives:

- local authorities: members and officers responsible for planning, environmental and regeneration policies – since they provide the framework within which others operate;
- the private sector: landowners, tenants, and particularly developers who have the opportunity to incorporate green design principles into their developments from the start;
- local communities whose contribution is critical to effective design and the sustainability of initiatives;
- staff and board members in regeneration partnerships, for whom environmental enhancement is a necessary condition of success;
- those in environmental organisations who provide advice and support for local activities.

Much of the guide is concerned with the design, planning and management of amenity open space. But the scope is wider, and we want the design principles, approaches, and management arrangements described here to influence how other types of green space are conceived and constructed – the landscapes around industrial sites for example – so that their functions can be expanded to include conservation of biodiversity, community development, or both.

The case studies confirm that there is already substantial 'greening' activity taking place – though by no means everywhere. The Guide therefore:

- explores the importance of greening activities, and describes the benefits;
- presents guidance on developing a strategic planning framework for greening initiatives;
- provides advice on local action to plan, implement, manage, maintain and monitor greening projects;
- offers suggestions on how to develop the partnerships so critical to the success of greening, and on involving local communities.

Greening the City: Guide to Good Practice

2 Why urban greening?
– Objectives and benefits

2.1 Introduction

The promotion of urban greening has acquired significance recently for a number of different interest groups with a variety of objectives. Indeed there is almost no area of environmental, social or economic policy towards which greening is not held to make a significant contribution.

Certainly the range of greening initiatives is diverse, and the case for urban greening can be made on different levels. While no project can satisfy every possible objective, the case studies suggest that good projects can tackle a number simultaneously. Urban greening has an important contribution to make to sustainable development which has economic, environmental and social components. Figure 3 provides some specific examples.

The Black Country Development Corporation recognised 'the need for a landscape framework that could be implemented as an integral component of its overall strategy for regeneration.'

John Lacey, Black Country Development Corporation

Figure 3: The potential benefits of urban greening

Economic regeneration
- improved image helps inward investment and business retention;
- positive publicity for businesses;
- facilities for employees;
- direct employment opportunities;
- attracting tourism;
- contributes to sustainable development.

Environmental
- supporting plant and animal communities;
- pollution control;
- influencing micro-climates;
- support biodiversity;
- recharging ground water levels;
- reduce problems of soil erosion;
- better urban greenspace reduces journeys to and pressures on the countryside.

Educational, social and cultural
- improved leisure and sports facilities;
- better understanding of nature and the environment;
- enhanced well-being through contact with nature;
- healthier life-styles;
- improved self-image, self-esteem and confidence for communities;
- stronger, better integrated communities.

2.2 Greening and economic regeneration

The relationship between economic regeneration and the environment is complex. On the one hand, it is argued, since economic regeneration requires the consumption of resources, it can never be secured without environmental damage. But equally, it is held (by most of our case study managers, among many others) that a clean and attractive environment is a key prerequisite for economic development.

However, environmental conditions by themselves are rarely sufficient to influence companies' location or investment decisions. Indeed for many of the cases reviewed for this Guide, the driving policy imperative was economic regeneration, to which the environmental improvements were contributory factors. But a clear message from the cases is that the prospects of job creation and retention are damaged by a poor environment and image. Greening is therefore a necessary, albeit not the only, component of successful regeneration strategies. An important lesson from the case studies underlines the need to integrate greening and green concerns at the core of the regeneration strategy, rather than adding environmental improvements as a cosmetic afterthought.

> '*The influence of a good natural environment will be more strongly felt if standards are more consistent throughout an urban area and if housing, industry and transport are set within a green framework.*'
>
> *Sustainability in Practice, English Nature, 1994*

The case studies illustrate how greening initiatives can contribute to economic regeneration objectives in a variety of ways. For example:

- the **Black Country Canals** programme (Case 1.1) not only improved the area's image, but formed a key part of an integrated programme of reclamation and new infrastructure to open up otherwise inaccessible land for development and comprehensive regeneration;

- the landscape improvements in **NUVIL** (New Uses for Vacant Industrial Land, Knowsley) (Case 3.2), although part of a wider package of regeneration measures, were decisive in attracting at least three businesses to the area;

- at the **Premier Business Park**, Walsall, (Case 4.1), a comprehensive masterplan which included planting, security measures and landscaping helped retain businesses (and therefore jobs) on the site; but in addition Groundwork Black Country introduced a programme of environmental audits for businesses leading directly to energy and waste efficiency savings.

2.3 Environmental and ecological benefits

Greening initiatives by definition generate environmental improvements. However, in practice there are significant variations in the quality of environmental benefits in greening activities. The cases show an imaginative range of options beyond shaved lawns and lollipop trees. Planning within a strategic framework, based on a comprehensive assessment and understanding of local conditions, can enhance and extend the range (and sustainability) of the environmental benefits to be derived from greening activities, including:

- the adoption of indigenous/'natural' landscapes which are usually cheaper both to introduce and maintain;

- the creation of wildlife corridors by establishing linkages between green spaces;

- the protection or establishment of habitats through sympathetic design frameworks.

Greening the City: Guide to Good Practice

**Figure 4: Amoco's Gas Terminal:
Designing in good environmental practice**

Amoco's commitment to the environments in which it works stems from its 'total quality management' philosophy. At Teesmouth the company worked closely with English Nature to protect the National Nature Reserve and SSSI within which its terminal sits, in a variety of ways:

• extensive site survey work to identify priorities for preservation;

• arranging piling schedules to avoid disturbing nesting birds;

• designing a rain water soakaway as a mini wetland;

• selecting a gravel size which encourages ringed plovers to nest;

• where safety regulations allow, restricting mowing regimes to encourage wild flowers.

Source: Case 4.2

The last two in particular can make positive contributions to the Government's commitment to the conservation of biodiversity.

One of the main objectives of Greening the City is to show how adopting environmentally sensitive principles of landscape design and management can enhance not only amenity space, but other landscapes too. It is now common practice to 'green' industrial parks – but with little thought for the ecological consequences or sustainability of the design. The **Amoco Gas Terminal** project, Teesmouth (Case 4.2), demonstrates how a range of nature conservation and environmental objectives can be achieved, provided respect for local conditions and good environmental practice are designed in from the beginning.

'If urban greenspace policies acknowledge the social and educational assets of accessible natural greenspace, then its inheritance value is seen to be unrivalled.'

John Handley, Groundwork Professor of Land Reclamation, University of Manchester

2.4 Educational, social and cultural benefits

The aims of regeneration are not exclusively economic. The Single Regeneration Budget Challenge Fund includes a range of objectives which, cumulatively, contribute to the 'quality of life'. In addition to environmental and economic regeneration, almost all our case study projects address wider regeneration objectives, both in what they seek to achieve, and, perhaps more importantly, how they seek to achieve them. Almost all stress the importance of working with local communities, in deciding the strategy, drawing up design principles, and very often, in implementation and management as well. Involving local people is not restricted to greening projects: it is a feature of all regeneration activity. But these cases suggest that the prospect of becoming involved in shaping the surrounding environment may strike a chord with many people in a way that other regeneration projects do not. Greening activities may offer a particularly effective way to engage local people, and thus contribute to the development of more cohesive communities.

The need to involve local people in environmental initiatives is a core element of 'sustainable development'. The key document to emerge from the Rio Earth Summit, known as 'Agenda 21', stressed the role of local authorities and the importance of

Figure 5: Whitmore Primary School

A variety of activities stimulated by WAGE – the Whitmore Action Group for the Environment include:

- tree planting in and around the school;

- creation of bee and butterfly areas protected by hazel hurdles made by the children;

- living willow tunnel structures;

- production of the Little Green Magazine, circulated to every primary school in the borough;

- wildlife watch club.

Source: Case 5.3

action at the local level. Engaging communities in planning and implementing greening initiatives can provide a focus for Local Agenda 21 programmes, as we discuss later.

Only one of the case study projects is explicitly educational (**Whitmore School**, Hackney, Case 5.3), but using greening projects as an educational resource is a common theme running through many of them: an explicit objective of the Black Country Development Corporation's (BCDC) landscape strategy is the creation of natural habitats within school grounds. In **Kings Cross Estate Action** (Case 2.2), schoolchildren were involved in designing a playground, and at a later stage in the project, will be involved in carrying out a planting scheme. The **Cramlington Organisation for Nature and the Environment** project (CONE), (Case 5.4), has established a series of wildlife areas in schools which offer a variety of links into the National Curriculum.

'Each local authority should enter into a dialogue with its citizens, local organisations and private enterprises and adopt a Local Agenda 21.'

Earth Summit, Rio, 1992

The **Ridgeacre** Branch Canal (Black Country Canals, Case 1.1) project is one example of the BCDC strategy in operation. As with the CONE project, Ridgeacre has set out to create an educational resource linking into the National Curriculum. A programme known as GreenIT has been developed jointly by Groundwork and Dudley Education Authority, and sponsored by RTZ-CRM.

The activities developed at **Whitmore Primary School** (Figure 5) have initiated environmental and nature conservation projects at the heart of an inner London borough.

Finally, the case studies show the range of social and cultural benefits which flow from greening initiatives. At the simplest level, many of the projects have created amenity, leisure and recreation resources from dereliction – communities have gained (or in some cases, as in **Bold Moss** in St Helens, Case 3.6, regained) access to improved greenspace. But the human and community benefits of environmental improvements extend beyond the provision of amenities.

For some, access to open greenspace, and particularly in its natural state, is a fundamental component of 'well-being'. For example: '...the need for something green and wild, or a place to go for sanctuary or solitude, a place to experience 'derness' in the city, ...lie at the heart of the livable city'.[1] The relationship between natural or

---

[1] T Elkin, D McLaren, M Hillman: *Reviving the City: towards sustainable urban development* (Friends of the Earth, 1991)

Greening the City: *Guide to Good Practice*

wild landscape and human well-being is one of the key themes of urban greening identified by English Nature. An assumption underlying many nature conservation strategies and local plans is a link between ready and regular access to greenspace, and health through reduced stress levels.

It is increasingly accepted that one of the requirements for the regeneration of our most disadvantaged areas is an improvement in image, not just in the eyes of outsiders, but more importantly, from the perspective of those who live there. There is a close relationship between the environmental quality, and hence image, of a place, and the self-esteem and confidence of its residents. As long ago as 1964 the Civic Trust drew attention to the '...derelict land mentality', which it observed to be associated with physical dereliction.

Improving image as part of raising local confidence and self-esteem was one of the issues addressed by the development of the **Springfield Community Garden** in Bradford (Case 2.3), see Figure 6.

Figure 6: Springfield Community Garden

A community-driven project, the garden offers:

- allotments;
- formal gardens and ponds;
- rough play area for children;
- cash crop areas.

Beneficiaries include:

- pupils at a school for children with learning difficulties;
- local residents gaining access to horticulture training;
- local residents – through (among other things) advice on diet and home economics.

Benefits have included:

- a much improved image associated with increased pride among residents;
- reduced vandalism;
- volunteering as a first step back to productive activity for the long-term unemployed.

Source: Case 2.3

Key lessons
– Why urban greening?

- with thoughtful design, greening projects can address a range of objectives simultaneously;

- by themselves environmental improvements may not stimulate economic regeneration – but they are essential components of comprehensive strategies;

- greening projects can offer a means of promoting other 'green' measures, such as energy conservation or waste reduction, which have measurable benefits for participants, and help secure private sector commitment to greening;

- good design principles and a strategic framework can extend the range of environmental benefits of greening – for example through establishing wildlife corridors or protecting habitats – often at no extra cost;

- greening projects provide an effective way to engage local communities and thus contribute to community development;

- environmental improvements make a significant contribution to the image of an area – and hence the quality of life and confidence of those who live and work there.

Greening the City: *Guide to Good Practice*

3 Developing a strategy

3.1 Introduction

The last Chapter looked at why urban greening is important and the benefits it brings. The next four chapters examine how to introduce and maintain greening initiatives, focusing on:

- developing greening strategies;
- planning and implementing projects;
- managing and maintaining greening initiatives;
- building support, involving local communities and developing partnerships.

Although our review of current practice focused largely on local projects and initiatives, we were keen to relate them to their strategic context. In most cases projects arise from, or are clearly influenced by, wider strategies (for example **Sheepwash Urban Park**, Case 3.4, **Southampton Greenways**, Case 1.2 or **Black Country Canals**, Case 1.1). In some cases projects succeed in (and despite) the absence of a broader strategy. There are also examples where the project has stimulated or influenced wider strategy design.

But it is important to establish greening initiatives within a strategic framework for a variety of reasons:

- environmental improvements are only likely to exert real influence on wider regeneration if they are an integral part of, and have systematic links to, a comprehensive strategy which addresses other regeneration goals;
- as development erodes open space, isolated green islands emerge: a green planning framework is needed to link green space, to provide wildlife corridors;
- potential uses vary and may lead to conflicts which a planning framework can resolve (for example balancing access and conservation);
- promoting a response to the character of place which creates diversity, variety and sustainability, through the use of design standards;
- nature conservation and protection principles need to be integrated into land use planning.

Many local authorities now claim to have – or to be developing – 'green plans' but it is not clear whether these can be implemented, or how far they feed into corporate local authority practice and the statutory planning framework.

If scarce resources for environmental improvements are to be used to maximum effect, if local authorities and their partners are to respond adequately to Local Agenda 21, (and to the challenges of the local Habitat Action Plans and Species Action Plans demanded by the UK Biodiversity Action Plan), and if the philosophy of greening is to inform the way our towns are managed, there needs to be:

- a systematic approach to the development of strategies influencing environmental improvement (including land use, open space, nature conservation);
- a commitment to incorporate these priorities in the Local Plan or Unitary Development Plan and local planning briefs and design guidance;
- mechanisms which ensure local projects reflect (and influence the continued development of) the statutory planning framework.

A model process, both for the development of the strategic policy framework, and its implementation at local level is set out in Figure 7.

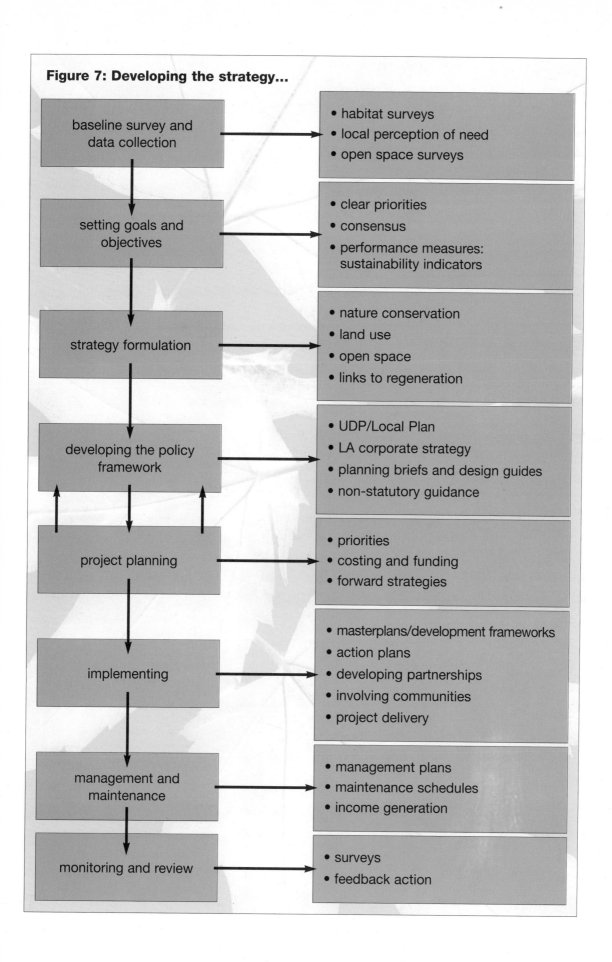

Figure 7: Developing the strategy...

baseline survey and data collection	• habitat surveys • local perception of need • open space surveys
setting goals and objectives	• clear priorities • consensus • performance measures: sustainability indicators
strategy formulation	• nature conservation • land use • open space • links to regeneration
developing the policy framework	• UDP/Local Plan • LA corporate strategy • planning briefs and design guides • non-statutory guidance
project planning	• priorities • costing and funding • forward strategies
implementing	• masterplans/development frameworks • action plans • developing partnerships • involving communities • project delivery
management and maintenance	• management plans • maintenance schedules • income generation
monitoring and review	• surveys • feedback action

Greening the City: *Guide to Good Practice*

3.2 Baseline survey and data collection

A prerequisite for the development of a greening strategy – as for any other kind – is an analytical and mapping exercise to help identify priorities for action, and to provide a baseline against which to measure subsequent progress. Many of the case studies have involved physical assessments (**Southampton Greenways**, Case 1.2, **Black Country Canals**, Case 1.1, **Sowe Valley**, Coventry, Case 5.2). But in most cases the mapping exercise should encompass the perceptions and priorities of local communities – for example in **Kings Cross Estate Action** (Case 2.2) a Planning for Real exercise was conducted at the start.

Examples of the mapping activities undertaken in the 'state of the environment' assessments include:

- habitat survey: the categorisation of under-developed land by habitat type (**Southampton Greenways**, Case 1.2), using an approach developed by the Joint Nature Conservation Committee, which allows for cross boundary comparisons;

- environmental audit: Dudley Metropolitan Council have prepared an audit covering soil, water and air pollution, with information on land use, recreation and nature conservation.

- landscape assessments: in Coventry and Leicester the local authorities assessed the qualitative aspects of the landscape: see Figure 8.

Figure 8: Landscape Survey, Sowe Valley, Coventry

- land use and character;
- the intensity and nature of use;
- access both by foot and car;
- circulation and accessibility by different categories of users;
- landscape features including field boundaries and mature trees;
- natural history;
- opportunities for introducing new planting to screen intrusive development on the fringes of the valley, for increasing accessibility and removing eyesores;
- opportunities for exploiting the recreational and educational potential;
- opportunities to encourage greater natural diversity and increase the nature conservation value;
- conflicts between uses and functions.

Source: Case 5.2

In some cases, the assessments have been used as the base for detailed land-use classifications, for example:

- important green corridors, wedges and open spaces;
- areas of nature conservation and social value;
- areas of deficiency and/or opportunity;
- threats to the landscape (physical and natural);
- the establishment of environmental performance indicators to measure the impact of any change.

3.3 Setting goals and objectives

Over the last 15 years, a major contributor to the development of good practice in greening has been the Groundwork movement, whose 43 local trusts are active in the design and implementation of environmental improvement projects across the country. Figure 9 summarises the lessons of the Groundwork experience.

Figure 9: The lessons of Groundwork experience

- A strategic approach which addresses local needs, is supported and valued by local people and which fits in with and complements the strategy of the local authority.

- Local 'ownership' of the vision, the strategy, any paid staff, the projects and the finances, in other words local management to high professional standards.

- A long term commitment and a sense of permanence to reflect the fact that greening and growing are continuous processes and that the communities which stand to benefit will likewise evolve and change. Managing and adapting greenspace over time is just as important as creating it in the first place.

John Davidson, Chief Executive, 1996

A critical element in the development of a locally owned, long-term strategic approach is the establishment of clear goals and objectives, reflecting the priorities identified in the baseline assessment. The goals must be:

- ambitious enough to make a difference, but achievable – preferably offering the prospect of some short-term success;

- part of a widely supported strategy, and its objectives must reflect a vision with which a wide range of partners can identify;

- acceptable to the local communities they are designed to benefit;

- specific enough to shape priorities for action, but with the flexibility to change over time;

- measurable to enable progress to be monitored; with each objective having clear performance targets.

One example of a clear statement of strategic aims is set out in Figure 10.

Figure 10: Blackbrook Valley Strategy, Dudley

- to conserve and enhance the existing landscape and drainage of the Valley;

- to minimise the impact of development/redevelopment on the ecology of the Valley by identifying and protecting areas of special natural importance and by taking ecological principles into account in the design and management of the Valley as a whole;

- to ensure that management proposals for the Valley are defined in the context of the design of landscape treatments;

- to encourage the use of the area as an educational resource;

- to use the landscape improvements survey and environmental monitoring work in the Valley as a vehicle for increasing community involvement in decision-making, self help and long term management.

Source: Case 3.5

Greening the City: Guide to Good Practice

Attaching measurable performance indicators to objectives is important for any strategy, but especially so in the field of environmental improvements, because of Local Agenda 21, and the concept of 'sustainable development'. A number of UK local authorities are collaborating in the design of 'sustainable development indicators' (SDIs): measures of environmental performance which reflect the concerns of local people, and are relevant to long-term sustainability. The experience gained in the development of SDIs by the Leicester Environment City project is summarised in Figure 11.

Figure 11: Designing Sustainable Development Indicators

identify issues of local concern

- widespread consultation
- part of LA 21 process

choose indicators

- reflect data sources
- support case for improved data gathering
- draw on experience of other authorities

select data

- draw on existing sources
- widespread responsibility, but central co-ordination
- readily available and affordable data
- simple presentation

apply targets

- wherever possible
- quantified where possible
- involve those responsible for achieving targets in setting them

communicate indicators

- develop communication plan
- reflect the needs of target audiences
- establish mechanisms for community feedback

review indicators

- reflect changing community priorities
- reflect changed environmental circumstances

Source: Local Sustainability, (Leicester Environment City Trust, 1996)

3.4 Developing strategies – shaping policy

Greening activities touch a wide variety of concerns. The framework within which greening takes place in any area therefore needs to draw on and influence a range of strategies. For example the establishment of Groundwork Black Country in 1988 across four boroughs helped influence:

- The Black Country Urban Forestry Initiative (now the National Urban Forestry Unit): which provides an overall strategy for the delivery of urban forestry across the Black Country;

- The Black Country Nature Conservation Strategy: a co-ordinated approach to the conservation of the Black Country's natural resources;

- Black Country Development Corporation Landscapes Strategy: a unifying landscape strategy for the Corporation's area designed to create a positive identity, as an attractive framework for development.

'Without the right aims, planning will always be handicapped in its efforts to help achieve sustainability. Defining clear aims is crucial. It sets the process off in the required direction and provides the essential yardstick against which subsequent proposals and policies can be compared.'

Sustainability in Practice, English Nature (1994)

As Local Agenda 21 recognises, effective environmental strategies require collaboration by a wide range of partners (as we discuss in more detail in Chapter 6). Nevertheless, there is a central role for local authorities – principally because of their responsibilities in the planning process, but for other reasons too:

- their role in integrating open space planning with wider measures of environmental sustainability, economic and social development;

- their responsibility for appropriate design standards which reflect the character and function of a particular place/landscape;

- their role in ensuring that accessible open space/green areas are provided throughout the urban area and for all sections of the population;

- as the link between national and international policy objectives and local action on the ground;

- because they offer a framework within which a variety of organisations can work towards common goals.

One of the key issues concerns the extent to which the range of local environmental strategies discussed here feeds into the statutory planning process – for example as illustrated in Figure 12.

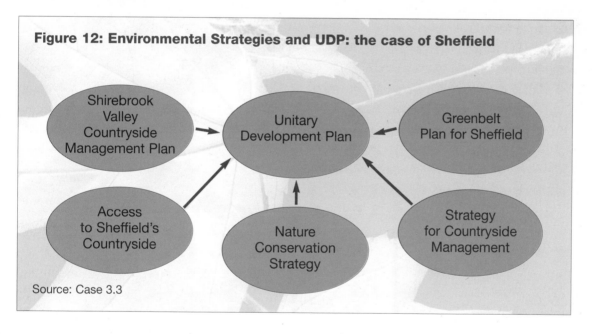

Figure 12: Environmental Strategies and UDP: the case of Sheffield

Shirebrook Valley Countryside Management Plan → Unitary Development Plan ← Greenbelt Plan for Sheffield

Access to Sheffield's Countryside → Unitary Development Plan

Nature Conservation Strategy → Unitary Development Plan

Strategy for Countryside Management → Unitary Development Plan

Source: Case 3.3

Greening the City: *Guide to Good Practice*

The implications of sustainable development mean that greening strategies need to extend beyond the provision of green areas and amenities. As the three local authority associations (the Association of County Councils, the Association of District Councils and the Association of Metropolitan Authorities) have recognised (among others), green issues now lie at the heart of the planning system. Their key recommendations for reform are set out in Figure 13.

Figure 13: Environment and the planning system

Specific reforms need to be introduced to entrench sustainable development at the heart of the planning system. In order to equip planning to play its role more effectively there is a need to:

- broaden the remit of 'material considerations' for development control purposes to include issues such as public health, the management of natural resources and energy;

- require authorities to develop sustainability reporting mechanisms covering their areas and make the results public;

- include in development plans objectives and targets (eg improvements to air quality levels, improvements to green space) which should be closely tied to corporate sustainability targets based on a State of the Environment report;

- strengthen project environmental assessment procedures and introduce mandatory strategic environmental assessment for plans, policies and programmes at both central and local government level;

- integrate the planning system better with 'quality of life' approach adopted through Local Agenda 21 initiatives.

Source: Environmental Manifesto for Local Government
(Local authority associations, 1996)

'Sustainable development is not just another name for environmental protection. It is concerned with issues which have long-term effects which are irreversible. A new approach to policy-making is required which does not trade off short-term costs and benefits but regards some aspects of the environment as absolute constraints.'

UK Local Government declaration on sustainable development 1993

Key lessons
– Developing a strategy

the importance of a strategic approach
- individual greening initiatives should be established within a strategic framework:
    - to ensure links to regeneration objectives
    - to promote physical links between green projects
    - to help determine priorities
    - to integrate greening principles into design standards and planning processes

baseline surveys and data collection
- strategy development should be based on detailed analytical and mapping exercises to identify priorities and provide a benchmark against which to measure progress;
- the exercise should normally include a review of the perceptions and priorities of local communities.

setting goals and objectives
- strategies need to establish clear goals which are:
    - ambitious but achievable
    - communicable
    - acceptable to local communities
    - measurable yet flexible
- all local authorities should establish local 'sustainable development indicators' which reflect local concerns.

developing strategies – shaping policy
- the local greening policy framework should take account of a variety of strategies including nature conservation, landscape, forestry – as well as broader regeneration strategies;
- strategies must extend beyond greenspace and amenity – incorporating sustainable development issues;
- greening strategies must inform the statutory planning framework, influencing District and Unitary Development Plans.

Greening the City: Guide to Good Practice

4 Initiating, planning, financing and implementing projects

4.1 Introduction

The impact of a greening strategy depends on the effectiveness of local initiatives and projects. This Chapter reviews good practice in initiating, planning, financing and implementing greening projects.

The logical (and preferred) sequence in which strategies precede the development of projects which are then implemented and managed does not always apply in the real world. Projects may stimulate strategies – though in any case project development is an iterative process, and the same issues require constant attention throughout. Mechanisms for community consultation continue to be important during the implementation and management phases as well as planning and design. The timescales of these projects (many of which have been in development for well over a decade) inevitably means that fund-raising is also a continuous activity.

'the design and management of the growth of any landscape is a continuous and interactive process.'

Landscape Institute.[2]

4.2 Getting started

Whether projects or strategy comes first, why is it that in some areas there is a high level of environmental awareness and greening activity, whilst elsewhere in apparently similar circumstances, little appears to be going on? Chris Wood in a study for the Anglo-German Foundation[3] on greening derelict land, identifies two prerequisites for getting things started effectively:

- people or communities who will act as project 'animateurs';
- a vision and strategy by which the initiators' enthusiasms can be shared.

This analysis is very much confirmed by our cases. Almost every project and initiative depended, at least in its early stages, on the energies and commitment of individuals or a group. But the cases show that by itself that is not enough. There needs to be a communicable vision that secures co-operation and support from potential partners, funders, local politicians, and other key individuals and organisations.

4.3 Project planning and design

Greening is a long-term activity. Many of the projects in the case study section have been under way for years. Large-scale greening initiatives (**Bold Moss**, Case 3.6 or the **Sheepwash Urban Park**, Case 3.4) develop incrementally, often in response to the availability of funding. Project planning arrangements must be flexible therefore; but for precisely that reason a comprehensive management or master-plan is essential.

Developing successful greening is largely a function of project design. Key elements of the process include:

- consultation, participation and partnership: to increase understanding, knowledge and appreciation of the natural environment;
- resources, skills and techniques: to ensure environmental improvements are implemented effectively;
- good management and maintenance: to ensure environments are appropriately managed and maintained in an effective and co-ordinated way;

---

[2] quoted in *People, Parks and Cities* (HMSO, 1996)
[3] *The Greening of Derelict Land: Rehabilitation Policies in Britain and Germany* (Anglo-German Foundation, 1996)

- design principles for greening: which recognise the role of landscape design and set out principles for greening of the urban environment.

In addition to these general principles, there are four sets of specific planning and design issues which need to be taken into account:

- design in relation to function and use;
- access and accessibility;
- nature conservation;
- maintenance costs.

4.3.1 landscape design in relation to function and use

The case studies demonstrate a range of ways in which design can be matched to function.

In the **Kings Cross Estate Action** (Case 2.2), the designers used traditional, formal urban squares to provide contemporary uses and functions. The formal layout of mowed lawns and plane trees reflects the historic traditions of the area and the former status afforded to the squares, which were considered worth retaining. The needs of the community were diverse. Very young children wanted a play area, older children wanted a kick-about area, the elderly wanted quiet areas to sit, and dog owners wished to walk their dogs. The needs of the residents also conflicted with the uses made of the area by drug dealers, drinkers and prostitutes. With sensitive design, increased security, definition of public and private spaces and extensive community negotiation, the designers managed to incorporate multiple use areas, identify priority user areas and control usage by undesirable elements.

4.3.2 access and accessibility

If greening is to contribute to improved quality of life then greening strategies must ensure that green spaces are readily available to all – and, if they are to support other environmental objectives, within walking distance of the communities they serve. Middlesbrough BC has enshrined the principle of 'access for all' in its Space for Nature initiatives (Figure 14).

Figure 14: Greenspace for all: Space for Nature

By the turn of the century there will be an area of wildlife interest within 1km of every house.

The nature conservation plan protects 22 existing sites and proposes 10 new ones.

A new category of greenspace has been created – Local Naturespace based on:

- wildlife value;
- use of site by schools or local residents;
- proximity to areas of low income and car ownership.

Source: Middlesbrough BC Nature Conservation Plan

The Middlesbrough target is ambitious but still falls below standards of accessibility recommended by English Nature,[4] which suggests that everyone should have access to at least two hectares of natural green space within 280 metres.

---

[4] Harrison et. al.: *Accessible Natural Greenspace in towns and cities: A review of appropriate size and distance criteria* (English Nature, 1995)

Greening the City: Guide to Good Practice

Design must also reflect the special needs of particular groups, including ethnic minorities, women, the elderly, the young and those with disabilities. For example the **Neighbourhood Nature** initiative (Case 2.1) has specifically tailored its greening initiatives to the needs of a Bangladeshi Women's Group in the Walsall City Challenge area and has initiated special events to engage that community. The design of gates, interpretation boards, footways, sitting areas and the use of planting, have also reflected the needs of people with disabilities.

In practice accessibility is not just about proximity: it is also, crucially, to do with a sense of security about open space. Particularly where landscapes are naturalistic, and designed to preserve or create safe wildlife habitat. Design principles must also take into account human safety. Fear of crime may be a greater issue than crime itself.

The British Crime Survey has shown no statistical link between natural open space and risk of personal assault.[5] Nevertheless the sense of insecurity may be enough to discourage access. The English Nature research report referred to earlier, included recommendations on key elements of design strategies, summarised in Figure 15.

Figure 15: Removing fear of crime from open space

Improve sightlines and permeability of natural areas – an essential element in designing safer urban environments, by 'designing out' overgrown shrubbery and other thick barriers which could shield a potential attacker; close attention to entrances and exits into safe 'busy' areas improves the permeability of an area;

Reducing hiding and entrapment spots, defined as small, confined areas close to a well-travelled route without possibility of escape because they are enclosed on three sides; clear sight lines for long distances with paths of 4 metres minimum width; graded vegetation at paths edges and plantings including deciduous species improve feelings of safety;

Improve lighting – the major problem in public open space and has a fundamental effect on the extent to which people can read cues about strangers, and maintain surveillance.

Source: Accessible natural greenspace in towns and cities
(English Nature, 1995)

4.3.3 nature conservation

Most of our case studies originate from broad regeneration objectives, rather than nature conservation – but the best development, at whatever scale, works with natural conditions, not against them. The case studies demonstrate that it is perfectly possible to design in principles and approaches which maximise the benefits for wildlife, without compromising any of the other goals. Concern for nature conservation is important at two levels:

- the individual site or project;
- the strategic relationship between sites.

At the site level, many of the underlying design principles in relation to wildlife objectives resemble those arising more generally: are the nature conservation objectives consistent with the characteristics of the site, and the resources available to it? A study for English Nature identified the main reasons why habitat creation projects failed – a summary is reproduced at Figure 16.

---

[5] Mayhew, P and Maung, N A: *Surveying Crime: Findings from the 1992 British Crime Survey* (HMSO, 1992)

Figure 16: Reasons for habitat creation project failure

- project not thought out properly: precise objectives not set;
- project too ambitious for the time/resources available;
- soils not investigated adequately: inappropriate species/plant assemblages introduced;
- long term after-care not properly addressed;
- monitoring inadequate either to see if objectives have been met or to provide feedback which might be used to modify the project.

Source: Parker, Habitat Creation – a critical guide
    (English Nature, 1995)

It is also important to provide links between open spaces as 'wild-life corridors' to allow for the movement of species and avoid what have been characterised as 'genetic bottlenecks'. For example Chris Baines[6] has described how house-builders, by constructing a culvert over a stream, inadvertently blocked a movement corridor for kingfishers which do not fly through enclosed spaces. A recent study for English Nature confirmed the importance of corridors for some migratory species. The report's recommendations are set out in Figure 17.

Figure 17: Wildlife corridors

- corridors should be preserved, enhanced and provided, where this can be cost-effective, as they do permit certain species to thrive where they otherwise would not;
- corridors should be as wide and continuous as possible; and
- their habitat should match the requirements of the target species.

Source: Dawson, D., Are Habitat Corridors for Animals and Plans in a Fragmented Landscape?
    (English Nature, 1994)

4.3.4 maintenance costs

Long-term maintenance is an essential element of greening design, and of achieving value for money, particularly if resources are limited:

- pressures on budgets, and especially revenue spend, require cost-conscious design solutions: projects dependent on high maintenance requirements are likely to deteriorate;
- the fixed- or short-term character of most public funding regimes (the Urban Development Corporations, City Challenge, the SRB Challenge Fund) necessitates a clear focus on post-funding arrangements: a forward or exit strategy.

Design solutions – and therefore maintenance arrangements – must reflect the broad range of use discussed earlier (4.3.1). No landscapes are maintenance free, but a feature of many of the case studies, particularly those concerned with the reclamation of large areas (eg **NUVIL**, Case 3.2, or **Woodlands by the Motorway**, Case 1.3) was their use of techniques to accelerate 'natural' processes allowing indigenous landscapes to re-establish themselves, offering a number of advantages:

- a naturalistic approach, particularly if it is sensitive to existing features, helps produce variety and diversity of design;

---

[6] Chris Baines: *The Wild Side of Town* (BBC, 1986)

- natural landscapes are likely to afford high levels of habitat and species protection;
- encouraging the development of natural landscapes is likely to require less resources than more formal designs and is thus consistent with the principles of sustainable development which require minimal and efficient resource utilisation;
- the 'naturalistic' landscape is likely to be cheaper to maintain.

The adoption of 'naturalistic' approaches is not always appropriate and should not be viewed as a low cost solution to all greening within the city. In any case, such areas still require careful and skilled management. There is also a need within the urban environment for a variety of open spaces including the highly maintained formal park and hard-landscaped areas.

Nevertheless, the use of low cost techniques can provide an excellent solution to large scale problems of dereliction and damage or as a temporary solution to sites awaiting redevelopment. There are massive areas of derelict, damaged or otherwise unused land in this country. The case studies demonstrate a range of cost-effective approaches which do not threaten the ultimate economic value of the land. For example:

- the **Sowe Valley** project (Case 5.2) where large scale gang mown areas have been replaced with woodland;
- **Bold Moss**, (Case 3.6) with its emphasis on encouraging natural recovery through a 'soft engineering' approach embedded in landscape management plans.

One indication of the widely varying costs of a range of landscape solutions is provided by a study commissioned by the National Urban Forestry Unit, which shows the maintenance costs of different types of woodland schemes compared with grasslands (Figure 18).

Figure 18: Grassland and woodland maintenance

	Average annual costs (£/ha)	
	Years 1 – 9	Years 10 – 50
Amenity grassland 50% mown by hand	2,220	2,220
Amenity grassland 10% mown by hand	1,690	1,690
'New Town' style woodland	1,040	1,220
Woodland in urban parks	980	720
Meadow grassland	760	760
Rough grassland	622	620
Naturally colourising woodland	360	530
Pioneer style woodland	300	550

Source: Urban Woodland and Grassland Comparative Management Costs, LUC (NUFU, 1996.)

A study undertaken by the University of Liverpool[7] examined four inner city greening schemes:

- one adopted an 'engineering' approach, which disregarded site characteristics by importing topsoil and using large tree planting stock;
- the other three adopted an ecological approach – adapting to site conditions, with small tree planting stock arranged in mass plantings.

[7] Michael, N et. al.: A Comparison of Different Approaches to Landscape Establishment in Urban Areas (University of Liverpool, 1993)

The second type of scheme cost about 10 per cent of the first; had significantly lower maintenance costs; produced as satisfactory a landscape in as short a time; and demonstrated less tree damage.

There are powerful arguments in favour of landscapes which show a natural response to the environments in which they are located. But they may not suit everyone's taste or expectations. To some, and particularly those whose experience of green space largely derives from formal parks, close mown paths and edges may be necessary as an indication of care and stewardship.

4.4 Funding

The scale of the case study projects varies, and so too do funding requirements – but there are common features. There is increasing pressure on budgets, especially for local authorities. Indeed the finance arrangements for a number of the case studies are the product of a search for alternative ways of financing greening activities which once may have been provided through local authority core services.

One potential alternative source is the National Lottery, at least for some types of greening schemes. The Heritage Lottery Fund has earmarked substantial resources under its 'Urban Parks Programme'. Assistance may also be available from the Millennium Fund, although as with other types of National Lottery funding, support is generally restricted to capital spend. One particular Millennium programme, which can support site acquisition and preparation, design and establishment costs (up to a maximum of 50%) is Millennium Greens (Figure 19).

Figure 19: Millennium Greens

The Millennium Commission has agreed to award up to £10 million in grant to the Countryside Commission towards a £20 million programme which will enable at least 250 communities in England to have their own Millennium Green by the year 2000.

A Millennium Green is an area of open space, to be enjoyed permanently by the local community. A Millennium Green may be located in or on the edge of a city, town, suburb, village or hamlet. It may be very small or perhaps as large as 30 acres and is within easy walking distance of people's homes. Each Millennium Green has its own character – there may be trees, bushes, ponds, streams, paths. It is a place where people can relax, children can play and everyone can enjoy nature. Millennium Greens are permanent 'breathing spaces' for people of all ages.

Source: Countryside Commission

English Partnerships (EP) offers another possible source of finance for certain types of environmental project. For example, in the year to March 1996, the EP Investment Fund helped regenerate 1500 hectares of vacant, derelict or contaminated land. This fund requires support from at least one additional partner, but EP can also use its Land Reclamation Programme to fund projects which are not likely to secure private sector support. These are mainly aimed at creating attractive and safe local environments. EP estimates that up to £70m will be spent on projects with soft end uses in the 1996-97 financial year.

A key issue for project funding concerns the timescales required to develop and implement environmental initiatives. The majority of our case study projects began in

Greening the City: Guide to Good Practice

the 1980s, since when many of the programmes which initiated the projects (the Urban Programme, Community Programme, Derelict Land Grant) have been superseded. There is no guarantee that the next ten years will not involve further changes on a comparable scale. Projects must therefore have the capability to adapt to the shifting emphasis of funding regime priorities without the initial strategic objectives being lost. Most of the case study projects depend on 'cocktail funding', at least partly reflecting their range of objectives. Multiple funding can be onerous for the project manager, since it usually requires a separate series of monitoring, accounting and reporting arrangements for each funder. But it has its advantages too. Spreading finance across a range of regimes and agencies helps defray the risks associated with changes in regime rules. It is highly improbable that, over a period of ten years or more, funding will be available in a steady stream. Approvals will cover particular phases, and the profile of funding necessarily affects the profile of activity. The sequence and speed of work are often driven by fund availability, not the requirements of the project plan. There may be advantages as well as disadvantages (Figure 20).

Figure 20: The consequences of phased funding

The Sheepwash project developed through a series of discrete stages, each with its own financial approval, with advantages and disadvantages:

- the need to justify funding bids at each stage has ensured the continued development of ideas and plans; but

- each phase has tended to become a project in its own right, with the danger that an incremental approach diverts attention from long-term aims.

Source: Case 3.4

Although capital budgets may be under pressure, the main concern in the case studies is for revenue finance, to support long-term management, maintenance and monitoring. As discussed earlier in the section on project design (4.3), the uncertainties inevitably surrounding long-term public revenue funding have led to an increasing concern to design in low cost maintenance wherever possible. But some of the case studies have succeeded in securing contributions to revenue costs either from the private sector, or from commercial spin-offs of greening:

- in the case of **Bold Moss** (Case 3.6), the National Coal Board provided an endowment of £0.5m in 1989, the income from which continues to help support maintenance costs;

- the developers of the **Bedfont Lakes** site (Case 3.1) have set aside a commuted sum for the council as a contribution to maintenance;

- the **Southampton Greenways** (Case 1.2) project has been financed in part through agreements made under Section 106 of the Town and Country Planning Act 1990 from developers who have built developments nearby: for example, a Housing Association has paid for pathways and fencing as part of a housing scheme;

- the **Business Environment Association**, Blackburn (Case 4.3) has secured contributions from companies in the Blackburn and Darwen area to the cost of environmental improvements, as part of a package which includes energy conservation and waste reductions which lead to savings;

- the production of wood chips and wild flower seed for commercial sale has contributed to revenue costs for the **NUVIL** project (Case 3.2).

4.5 Implementation

The case studies vary, by scale, degree of complexity and focus. Nevertheless, implementation arrangements show a number of common features:

- many of the projects reviewed began more than ten years ago – an underlying issue with important implications for planning and organisation;

- projects are more likely to be implemented by a partnership, than a single agency;

- funding is unlikely to come from a single source or under a single approval: cocktail funding, approved sporadically, is standard;

- a variety of approaches have been adopted to ensure adequate skills and expertise are available;

- local communities are usually directly involved with implementation.

The two most striking features of project delivery – the timescales and the range of partners – can create difficulties in project implementation. To provide sustained co-ordination over a long period under these circumstances, many of our cases display one or both of these features:

- a core organisation around which partner agencies assemble;

- a master plan which provides continuity of purpose, but which is flexible enough to absorb changes in circumstances over time.

In Chapter 6 we review partnership arrangements. In many cases there is a central role for the local authority, partly because of its planning responsibilities, partly because it has access to the professional skills needed, but often too because of its role as a landowner. Just as external partnerships are needed, there needs to be a sense of internal partnership within the authority, since an important feature of many of the cases is their dependence on inter-departmental and inter-disciplinary working (Figure 21).

Figure 21: Inter-disciplinary working
Sheepwash Urban Park

A cross disciplinary working party was established to manage the implementation and subsequent management of the project, comprising engineers, planners, landscape architects and ecologists from various departments within the Council. Although no department had specific overall responsibility for the project, the planning department, and in particular one officer, became responsible for the overall co-ordination and implementation of the various projects over its ten year life.

Source: (Case 3.4)

In other cases, either instead of or, as with **Bold Moss**, (Case 3.6) alongside the local authority, the support of an outside organisation has been sought, with a range of roles encompassing adviser, facilitator and organiser. Groundwork is centrally involved in a number of our case studies, and is an obvious candidate to play this role through one of its 43 local trusts. But other groups playing this kind of facilitation role include the British Trust for Conservation Volunteers, English Nature, the National Urban Forestry Unit and the private sector.

Where projects take ten or more years to develop, there are inevitably shifts of emphasis: indeed adaptability and flexibility emerge as important characteristics of successful projects. But to ensure that schemes retain the strategic focus with which they started, in the face of unavoidable changes in personnel, financial regimes and local priorities, an overall master plan or flexible planning framework is a prerequisite for effective organisation.

Key lessons
Initiating, planning, financing and implementing projects

- projects don't always arise from strategies: in some cases the project stimulates the development of strategy.

getting started

- most projects owe their origins to a committed individual, or group, acting as 'animateur';
- if the idea is to take root, there must be a communicable vision to secure wider support.

project planning and design

- the long-term nature of many greening initiatives makes a comprehensive masterplan essential;
- the design process must take into account:
  -consultation and participation
  -resources and skills for implementation
  -management and maintenance
- the principal design determinants are function and use including the needs of local communities;
- if greening is to improve quality of life, there must be unimpeded access for all, preferably within walking distance;
- design must reflect special needs – of women, ethnic minorities and people with disabilities; and ensure greenspace where people are safe and feel safe;
- wherever possible there should be 'green corridors' linking projects to allow for the movement of species;
- nature conservation objectives should be consistent with site characteristics, and available resources;
- provision for maintenance must be built in at the design stage;
- encouraging a 'natural' landscape often entails lower management and maintenance costs than more formal design.

funding

- the timescale for greening projects means that funding regimes frequently change or even disappear during their lifetime – projects need to be planned with the capacity to adapt to shifting priorities without losing sight of original goals;
- project managers need to develop the skills to secure and manage 'cocktail funding';
- the National Lottery offers a possible source of finance;
- developers and land-owners should be encouraged to provide endowments in advance as a contribution to maintenance costs.

implementation

- project implementation should include a variety of partners – though there needs to be a core organisation in the lead;
- there is a key role for local authorities – requiring inter-departmental and inter-disciplinary working;
- projects often benefit from an outside organisation (Groundwork for example) acting as adviser and facilitator;
- projects need flexibility to adapt to change – but within the framework of an overall masterplan.

5 Management, maintenance and monitoring

5.1 Introduction

Many of the case studies, in response to revenue constraints, have systematically attempted to incorporate low maintenance solutions at the design stage. These include for example, the replacement of mown grass areas with tree planting, or the adoption of 'ecological' rather than engineered approaches to implementation. There is however, a major, though not always recognised, distinction between maintenance and management. In DOE's 'People, Parks and Cities' the distinction was put thus: 'at least part of the current crisis in public parks is attributable to an imbalance between maintenance – which freezes development – and management involving change'.

What are the critical ingredients of the distinction? The management of greening initiatives and open space requires the flexibility to identify and respond to a range of issues as they develop over time, some to do with the landscape, others to do with circumstances surrounding its use, including:

'...too often parks are regarded as a legacy to be maintained rather than as an asset to be developed.'

Competitive Management of Parks and Green Spaces, Audit Commission, 1988.

- access and security;
- marketing and publicity;
- use and impediments to use;
- community involvement;
- education.

In contrast, maintenance involves a relatively clearly defined set of tasks, of the kind that may be expressed in a contract specification for compulsory competitive tendering (CCT).

5.2 Management

The substantial variations in the scale, scope and objectives of the case study projects inevitably lead to significant differences in managerial resources and requirements. Nevertheless, there is a range of common management issues which all projects have to address.

5.2.1 management structures

In most of the case study projects there is a dedicated body responsible for overseeing overall management. The composition of the bodies varies, though commonly user groups are involved as a matter of policy, and in many instances there is an underlying objective concerned with community development. Examples include:

- **Bedfont Lakes**, Hounslow, (Case 3.1) managed by the Bedfont Lakes Ecological Advisory Committee, which includes councillors, officers, user groups, and the developer;
- the **Ridgeacre Canal** (Black Country Canals, Case 1.1) Friends of Ridgeacre will guide the development of the canal, and include residents, user groups (eg anglers) a conservationist, representatives of local schools, the police and the residents' association;
- **Southampton Greenways**, (Case 1.2) Community Action Forums have been established as a focus for links to the council.

5.2.2 staffing

Again reflecting the diversity of the case study projects, there are wide variations in staffing arrangements – in respect of numbers, mix and form of employment. But running through most of the projects are two sets of distinctions:

- between paid staff and volunteers (although many projects make good use of both);
- in the case of paid staff, between direct employment (whether of a local authority or another managing agency) and the use of contractors appointed to specific tasks under CCT.

It is important to involve local communities, not simply through consultation, but more directly in the implementation of greening projects. Developing a sense of stewardship, and shared responsibility for the environment, are important aspects of Local Agenda 21 – all of which argues powerfully in favour of building volunteering into the arrangements for managing and maintaining green space.

Nevertheless, a constant stream of committed and appropriately skilled volunteers cannot always be taken for granted. There are some key management tasks which it is rarely possible to leave exclusively to volunteers or community groups – providing a sense of security for example: a critical determinant of the extent to which green space is used in practice by women and other vulnerable groups. The extent to which project management and maintenance depend on volunteers is a function of scale, and objectives. **The Royate Hill Local Nature Reserve**, Bristol (Case 1.4) Bradford's **Springfield Community Garden** (Case 2.3) and the **Hillsborough Walled Garden** Sheffield, (Case 5.1) all depend, to a greater or lesser extent on volunteers reflecting the strong community dimension to all three.

The key issues surrounding the use of volunteers and community groups are to do with the maintenance of quality and standards, and the development of appropriate skills. A number of the projects demonstrate effective arrangements for skills development among volunteers:

- in the case of **Ridgeacre**, (Black Country Canals, Case 1.1) British Trust for Conservation Volunteers 'skill providers' work alongside volunteers, to help develop skills appropriate to the effective implementation of environmental projects;
- National Urban Forestry Unit has provided advice and guidance, including the distribution of leaflets on tree planting and aftercare, in the **Neighbourhood Nature** project (Case 2.1);
- at **Bold Moss**, (Case 3.6) training for volunteers (including a National Vocational Qualification Level II in Environmental Conservation) is available through Groundwork St Helens, Knowsley and Sefton.

There is an important contribution to be made by local people and their organisations which can also assist community development objectives. But in almost every case, the recruitment of volunteers, and arrangements for managing volunteer labour effectively and in accordance with quality standards, depends upon the availability of core staff (Figure 22).

Although it may not be practicable for every project under all circumstances, from our case studies those which appear to be most effective in responding to user requirements, in attracting users from a wide range of groups, and in being able to adapt to changing circumstances and demands, are those with core staff teams.

> **Figure 22: Core Staff and Community Involvement:**
>
> The Sowe Valley project in Coventry provides a good example of effective officer-volunteer collaboration.
>
> As the project has evolved community involvement in the project has increased, promoted by the two field officers and the Council. Their roles have changed from initiator and implementor to facilitator and enabler. The Sowe Valley Project has provided the strategic framework within which community action can develop. One example of such involvement is the creation of community woodland at Cremblett. As with many of the projects, an established residents association approached the field officer. They wished to improve the nature conservation value of a playing field and meadow adjacent to Callidin Castle Comprehensive School. The field officers assisted the Community in the design of the area and helped them to access funds that the Council would not have been able to access themselves. Some £5,000 was raised from English Nature, Shell Better Britain, and the Countryside Project.
>
> Source: Sowe Valley (Case 5.2)

Specific examples of how the availability of a ranger or warden service has led to good practice include:

- **Bold Moss** (Case 3.6) where a Community Link Officer was the key to a high level of community involvement and management arrangements to secure maximum possible local direction;
- **Saltwells Wood** Dudley (Case 3.5), where the presence of wardens has facilitated a responsive and flexible management style, significantly reducing vandalism and littering.

5.3 Maintenance

The maintenance (as opposed to the management) of local authority green space is subject to compulsory competitive tender (CCT). The DOE study on urban parks identified some improvements to the management and maintenance of parks resulting from CCT, many of which apply to green space more generally:

- creating inventories of open space;
- the need to think systematically about objectives for the use of space and how to achieve them, as the basis for drawing up tender specifications;
- greater public debate about the use of open space;
- increased transparency of management and maintenance costs;
- savings achieved – although not always returned to the overall open spaces budget.

Compulsory competitive tendering applies only to maintenance and not to the management of green space, and the warden or ranger functions are therefore not covered. Although it is possible to maintain directly employed wardens alongside tendered maintenance contracts, many local authorities, in the interests of keeping costs to a minimum, expect competitively tendered maintenance contracts to be sufficient by themselves. However, there are now examples where authorities are seeking to introduce (or restore) a warden service, in addition to maintenance arrangements determined through CCT.

For example, the **Sowe Valley** project (Case 5.2) was designed to keep management and maintenance costs to a minimum – by replacing gang mown areas with community woodland. Responsibility for management and maintenance is split,

Greening the City: Guide to Good Practice

between Coventry's Countryside Project, and the city's grounds maintenance contractor. Officers are exploring ways to fund a local ranger service to provide:

- more direct contact with local users;
- a greater capacity to respond to changing user requirements;
- greater control of vandalism and anti-social behaviour;
- monitoring of schemes.

5.4 Monitoring

In the management of environmental initiatives, as in any other area, there are certain prerequisites for effective monitoring:

- objectives defined with sufficient clarity to support measurable indicators of performance;
- a baseline position to give meaning to monitoring information;
- adequate staff resources to collect, analyse and respond to data.

Chapter 2 indicated the breadth of objectives embraced by greening projects. Effective project management requires a comparably broad range of performance indicators. However, projects have tended to concentrate principally on the environmental outcomes of their activity. Measurement of the other dimensions, if undertaken at all, tends to be restricted to a few fairly limited indicators (number of volunteers, school-children participating). One example of a relatively wide range of performance indicators, adopted by National Urban Forestry Unit for the **Woodlands by the Motorway** project (Case 1.3), is set out in Figure 23.

Figure 23: NUFU Performance Indicators

- timber output increment: turnover from woodland planting/production;
- vandalism: number of incidents;
- community involvement: number of meetings and numbers of people consulted;
- atmospheric pollution: the reduction of ambient levels of gaseous and particulate pollution;
- bio-diversity indicators: currently being developed by NUFU mainly in relation to gardens in terms of numbers and types of species and habitat variety;
- value for money: capital and life cycle cost of different types of greening;
- employment generation: through indirect impacts.

Source: Case 1.3

Increasingly, the context in which project performance monitoring takes place is Local Agenda 21. As we discussed earlier (Chapter 3) local authorities are encouraged to develop local sustainable development indicators which cover many of the measures of performance which individual greening projects would wish to monitor. In Leicester, experience of the Environment City project led to the identification of four key stages:

- understanding 'where we are now': gathering the baseline data;
- setting goals or targets for improvement;
- data gathering to illustrate progress towards targets;
- information on progress widely and effectively communicated.

This could serve as a model of good monitoring practice for any environmental improvement project.

Key lessons
— Management, maintenance and monitoring

- projects should recognise the key distinction between the maintenance of greenspace and its management which is concerned with the development of projects over time;

- issues of greenspace management include:
  - -access and security
  - -marketing and publicity
  - -use and impediments to use
  - -community involvement
  - -education

- wherever possible project management bodies should be partnership based, and include user groups and local communities;

- involving communities in project management can help foster the sense of environmental stewardship which underpins Local Agenda 21;

- management cannot be left exclusively to volunteers;

- projects should build in provision to develop volunteers' skills;

- for many projects, a dedicated warden or ranger service is crucial to good management;

- the effective monitoring of environmental projects require:
  - -clearly defined and measurable objectives
  - -a baseline position
  - -resources to collect, analyse and respond to information.

Greening the City: Guide to Good Practice

6 Building support for greening
– Involving local communities and developing partnerships

6.1 Introduction

Partnership working arrangements, and particularly those involving local communities, lie at the heart of most contemporary regeneration activities, and greening is no exception. The advantage of partnership structures in environmental improvement initiatives includes:

- the need to managing cocktail funding;
- having access to diverse skills and experience;
- encouraging the sharing of risk;
- providing a mechanism for securing community views;
- developing collective responsibility for environmental issues.

In practice, developing effective partnerships, and finding mechanisms which genuinely secure the involvement of local communities is not easy. This Chapter reviews the experience of our case study projects, and elsewhere, to offer guidance on:

- securing community involvement;
- building partnerships.

'Challenge Fund bids must be supported by partnerships (including) the private and public sector, local voluntary and community organisations including faith communities.'

The Challenge Fund: Bidding Guidance (DOE, 1995)

6.2 Securing community involvement

The critical importance of involving communities in the process of project development was stressed by almost all the project managers, and a common theme in discussions at our seminars. Consultation with local residents is a required feature of all current government-funded regeneration activity – indeed it is one of the criteria by which Challenge Fund bids are judged. But in the context of greening, community involvement now has a far greater significance than in other areas of regeneration activity, because of Local Agenda 21.

There are two features of LA 21 in particular which increase the significance of community involvement:

- LA 21 requires the involvement of local communities: it cannot be developed effectively by public authorities acting unilaterally;
- LA 21 embraces the broader notion of 'stewardship', a fundamental component of sustainable development: community involvement in greening is thus part of a process to develop collective responsibility for the environment.

Each of the case studies includes a description of the processes of consultation. The timing, extent and character of consultation does vary between projects, but in general it is clear that, in principle, consultation should begin as early as possible, covering the broadest possible range of issues and options, and should be relevant to the individuals being consulted. However, it has to be acknowledged that full and genuine consultation, in which community views are taken seriously, is not always welcomed or encouraged by professionals:

'Local Agenda 21 is about creating a plan for the future that is based on the widespread participation of local people and organisations'

Local Sustainability Leicester Environment City Trust, 1996

- it may involve extra cost – even if it can produce additional benefits later on;
- it can be time-consuming: for example there have been criticisms of the slow pace of progress on **Bold Moss** (Case 3.6) – because every step has been worked out with the local community;
- it may raise expectations which cannot be met.

Managing expectations is an issue; and doubtless there are variations in local circumstances which mean that extended, detailed consultation is not always appropriate. However, a number of the case studies demonstrate that it is possible to involve communities in all aspects of planning, design, implementation and management.

With greening, as with other aspects of regeneration, the professionals who need to be involved will not necessarily have experience of working with local communities. Some cases (for example **Bold Moss** Case 3.6) include a community development professional within the greening team – but this is relatively uncommon. Generally, landscape managers, parks and open space managers, and other professionals will need to develop an understanding of the types and techniques of community involvement.

There is extensive literature offering guidance on involving the community in regeneration activities, and it is beyond the scope of this guide to deal with the issue in detail. A variety of relevant publications is identified in the bibliography, including a recent DOE study on involving the community in regeneration.[8] However, there are two key issues to emerge from the case studies and other experience of involving local people in environmental improvement projects.

First, it is important to recognise that there is not a single community: managers of greening initiatives, as well as other regeneration projects, need to identify:

- the specific characteristics of local communities in the area;
- the distinctive needs of key groups (eg children, ethnic minorities, women, the elderly);
- a range of techniques for contacting and engaging with each.

Second, 'community involvement' can have a variety of meanings and meet a variety of objectives. These different objectives have been described as a 'ladder of involvement'[9], with five stages:

(i) information: a largely one-way flow from decision makers to the community;

(ii) consultation: comments are invited, usually on a limited range of options, though there is little community involvement in decision-making;

(iii) deciding together: joint decision-making involving the community and official agencies in tandem;

(iv) acting together: partnership-based management or delivery;

(v) independent community initiatives with official bodies playing an enabling role.

Although the appropriate level of involvement depends on the nature of the initiative, generally the good practice examples identified in the case studies are to be found towards the top of the ladder, at levels iii), iv) or v) for example.

- **Ridgeacre Canal**, Black Country (Case 1.1): a Planning for Real exercise generated a series of ideas which formed the basis for the management plan;
- the **Bold Moss** Forum (Case 3.6), brings together residents and councillors to oversee the design and management of the project;

[8] Department of the Environment: *Involving Communities in Urban and Rural Regeneration* (HMSO, 1995)
[9] Wilcox, D: *The Guide to Effective Participation* (Partnership, 1995)

- on the **Kings Cross Estates** (Case 2.2), the designers work iteratively with the community:

  -issues to be addressed are jointly identified;

  -designers produce outline ideas;

  -the community responds;

  -designers adapt their proposals.

- **Royate Hill Local Nature Reserve** (Case 1.4) residents, schools and local groups have helped reconstruct walls and fences, clear paths, and help with planting;

- in **Springfield Community Garden**, Bradford, (Case 2.3) all the work has been carried out with assistance from local volunteers – from the initial staking out to day-to-day maintenance.

Securing the involvement of the community, on any scale, is not always straightforward. In two of the case studies, community involvement was galvanised by threats to its amenities and environment, though this cannot be advocated. Techniques for engaging with communities demonstrated in these cases have included:

- reaching parents by involving children in activities;

- getting to user groups – for example at **Ridgeacre** (Case 1.1), Anglers' groups have been recruited to help with maintenance;

- employing staff with a specific community development function – at **Bold Moss** (Case 3.6), for example.

In larger or more formally organised projects, local communities should also be represented on partnership groups – though this should not be a substitute for wider involvement.

6.3 Building partnerships

Most of the case study projects have been implemented or managed by some form of partnership arrangement. Partnership groups reflect a range of funders: partly and through the need to engage users and local communities; partly because of LA 21 principles of shared responsibility.

There are significant variations in both the function and structure of partnership groupings in the case study projects:

- in the **NUVIL** project (Case 3.2) there is no formal partnership vehicle, although individual private sector companies are actively involved as partners in individual schemes;

- in the **Ridgeacre Canal** project (Case 1.1), an informal group, the Friends of Ridgeacre, has been established to oversee development. The group includes local residents, user groups and local professionals including a police officer and school-teacher;

- under the **Southampton Greenways** project (Case 1.2), there are 12 Community Action Forums which provide a link between local communities, via Community Action managers, to the council;

- in the **Shire Brook Valley** (Case 3.3), the Shire Brook Conservation Group was set up in 1989, since when its capacities have been developed by the public sector partners (Sheffield City Council, Forestry Authority, Countryside Commission) so that it now undertakes much of the maintenance and monitoring work.

These variations partly reflect differences in the projects themselves: but in some cases they may reflect a lack of clarity about the real role of the partnership. The Leicester Environment City Initiative has produced a useful analysis of its experience of developing and building partnerships – and being clear about the purpose of multi-sector partnerships is one of the key lessons. Others, which reflect the experience of the case studies, include:

- one organisation is usually needed to start the ball rolling – and independent, voluntary arm's length organisations are well placed – as illustrated by the role played by local Groundwork Trusts in a variety of examples, including **NUVIL** (Case 3.2), and the **Business Environment Association** (Case 4.3);

- successful partnerships are based round mutual gain – for example success of the **Premier Business Park** project (Case 4.1) reflects the mutual self-interest of the partners;

- although multi-sector partnerships are critical there is a unique role for local government: local authorities are involved, (in most cases centrally) in all the case studies, with the **Sowe Valley** (Case 5.2) and **Shire Brook Valley** (Case 3.3) projects demonstrating their catalytic role in partnership development;

- successful partnerships must involve the right individuals as well as the right organisations: many of the case study projects owe their origins to a committed individual – but projects sustainable over time depend on a careful blend of individuals;

- back up support helps partnerships succeed: many of the case study projects demonstrate the importance of professional staff time to secure maximum value form partnerships and volunteers. In the **Shire Brook Valley** (Case3.3), the staff resource was supplied by a council employee; in **Ridgeacre Canal** (Case 1.1), by British Trust for Conservation Volunteers; and in **Neighbourhood Nature** (Case 2.1), by NUFU.

Greening the City: Guide to Good Practice

Key lessons
– Building support for greening

involving communities

- partnership working, particularly involving local communities, is critical to greening activities;
- project managers need to identify the distinctive characteristics of local communities and ensure they adopt a range of techniques to reach different groups;
- in the context of LA 21 and sustainable development, community involvement is important as a way of developing 'stewardship';
- it is important to be clear about the purpose of community involvement;
- community consultation should begin as early as possible, and cover the widest possible range of issues;
- where possible, greening teams should include community development professionals.

building partnerships

- the purpose of partnerships should be made clear to all;
- partnerships usually require a stimulus to start them off;
- a core organisation and adequate resources are necessary for effective partnership working;
- it is important to involve the right individuals, as well as organisations;
- community representation in partnerships is no substitute for wider involvement.

7 Conclusions

Learning from experience

The good practice guidance in the preceding chapters is founded on the experience gathered from the case study projects that follow. The aim has been to ensure that the lessons from these projects, some of which were begun a decade ago, will contribute to the success of the greening schemes of the future.

The case studies demonstrate the wide variety of approaches to urban greening projects, as well as the marked differences in scale. Some are very ambitious and long-running projects, involving the reclamation of large tracts of derelict or vacant land (**NUVIL**, Case 3.2 or **Bold Moss**, Case 3.6). Others illustrate the value of modest greening schemes carried out on a neighbourhood scale; there is no reason, for instance, why any primary school should not replicate the example of **Whitmore School** (Case 5.3).

Most of the case studies are of greening projects with remedial objectives, designed to restore and regenerate existing but run-down environments. It is equally important that the principles which guided these projects are also applied to new-build schemes on greenfield sites and to the expansion of existing developments. Greening need not add to overall scheme costs, particularly if it is included in the initial design objectives, and may result in savings when maintenance costs are taken into account.

Thinking strategically

It is encouraging that a growing number of local authorities, together with their partners in the private sector and community generally, have begun to recognise the important role of greening in broader environmental strategies. If greening is to contribute to long term, comprehensive and sustainable regeneration, it must be fully integrated with regeneration strategies, not tacked on as a cosmetic afterthought. The Black Country Urban Forestry Initiative, the Black Country Nature Conservation Strategy, and the Black Country Development Corporation's landscape strategy all show how greening projects can form an integral part of the local regeneration strategies and statutory planning frameworks.

Recognising the benefits

This guide demonstrates the range of benefits to be gained from urban greening. Most obvious – as the 'before and after' pictures in the case studies show – is the visual transformation of the landscape that can be achieved through environmental improvements. This in turn can help improve the quality of life for people living and working in urban areas, with consequent benefits for their health and self-esteem. No less important is the contribution that changing the image of an area through environmental improvements can make to attracting inward investment as well as retaining existing businesses.

Well-informed and sensitive approaches to the design of greening schemes can also create habitats that contribute to bio-diversity and nature conservation (particularly if individual projects can be linked by a network of green corridors; **Southampton Greenways** Case study 1.2). In the longer term, greening schemes can also help to reduce the impact of other urban and environmental problems such as air pollution and noise.

It is this combination of economic, social and environmental benefit that makes greening a key component of schemes designed to satisfy criteria for sustainability and to meet the objectives set by Local Agenda 21.

Greening the City: Guide to Good Practice

Working in partnership

A feature common to most of the case studies is the role of partnerships in initiating, planning, funding and implementing greening projects, and in arranging effective management and after-care. The long time scale and multiplicity of funding sources sometimes required to implement greening schemes can represent a major commitment for a single organisation. A partnership approach allows the individual members to share workloads and responsibilities according to their capabilities, while maintaining a collective commitment to projects through to completion. The sense of achievement and ownership shared by the partners is likely to ensure that they will want to safeguard their investment for the future.

case studies

Contents

1.1 Ridgeacre Canal Project, Black Country

INTRODUCTION AND KEY ISSUES

Within their original strategy for the regeneration of the Black Country, the Black Country Development Corporation (BCDC), identified 16 km of canals as a priority area for investment in the environment. A strategy and action plan were prepared for the canal area in the context of a wider regeneration strategy for the Black Country. The strategy identified a number of sites which have subsequently been developed and have become the focus for new development, tourism and leisure activity. The Ridgeacre Canal project provides an example of one of the many projects that have been, or are currently being, implemented as part of the BCDC's canal strategy involving new development and the environmental enhancement of canals and their associated open spaces.

ACTION TAKEN

Strategic Planning

Landscape design and environmental enhancement of the Black Country was seen as an integral part of the BCDC's overall strategy for regeneration. A landscape strategy was devised for the BCDC area, comprising a series of initiatives, including:

- *urban forestry:* the establishment of urban forestry on public and private land using 'low-cost' techniques, involving a range of public/private partnerships;
- *canals:* the upgrading and improvement of 16 km of canal in partnership with British Waterways;
- *reclamation:* a co-ordinated approach to the reclamation of derelict land and integration of open space, woodland and habitat creation;
- *infrastructure and industrial enhancement:* environmental enhancement of key routes through the area in association with Groundwork's "Brightsite" initiative, which seeks to encourage industrialists to upgrade the environment of their premises;
- *nature conservation:* the protection and enhancement of nature conservation interests, whenever practicable;
- *advanced planting and structure planting:* key infrastructure and development sites;
- *education:* enhancement of school grounds/habitat creation;
- *community:* support for local community environmental initiatives.

The BCDC Landscape Strategy, together with the Black Country Nature Conservation Strategy (produced by the Black Country Boroughs and the BCDC) provided a co-ordinated and consistent approach to nature conservation and a robust framework for landscape and nature conservation within which more detailed projects/plans of action could be produced.

A series of Area Development Framework Plans (ADF's) produced by the BCDC provided the mechanism to translate strategic planning objectives into local plans of action.

Local Action

The Ridgeacre Branch canal lies north-east of West Bromwich town centre. The construction of the Black Country Spine Road across the canal allowed for the release of several areas of vacant land for development. The non-development land formed a linear green space connecting three residential areas to the town of West Bromwich. British Waterways wished to dispose of this land into Local Authority

Galton Valley

ownership. This was initially turned down, and Groundwork Black Country agreed to look at developing it for recreation and education purposes in conjunction with residents and industry in the surrounding the area. The project is programmed to run for three years at the end of which progress will be reviewed and the local authority may be able to 'purchase' the site with a well developed local management structure in place.

Community Involvement

Effective community involvement was seen as the key to the success of the project through obtaining new ideas, strengthening links between groups, implementing proposals and ensuring its long term success. The process of involvement commenced with a Planning for Real exercise, the results of which formed the basis of a series of area based projects, drawn up by Groundwork Black Country.

The projects, which are specifically designed to make the site safe, attractive, accessible and litter free, address some of the critical issues in the area, including health, training and employment, crime prevention, education, recreation and nature conservation. Groundwork have designed management plans for the site which identify the various projects, funding source(s), delivery agencies and phasing. The intention is to implement the projects with the local community and in the longer term, encourage the community to oversee the management of the site.

Tividale Quays

Education

A key element of the Ridgeacre project is its scope as an educational resource directly linked to the National Curriculum. A programme known as GreenIt, has been developed by Groundwork in consultation with Dudley Education Authority and sponsored by RTZ-CRM. It comprises a teaching pack designed to deliver various aspects of the National Curriculum. Children are encouraged to become involved in live projects with local private businesses. Through the programme pupils have a chance to learn about landscape design and other environmental topics and also interact with adults and other teachers.

A project has been developed at Ridgeacre with a local primary school. Through the GreenIt project pupils consider and suggest environmental improvements that could be made to the business premises along the canal. A series of activities including litter picks, environmental improvements, planting, art and construction, canal dipping and historical tours have been carried out.

FUNDING AND PARTNERS

Total capital cost for the project is estimated at £514,000 with £165,000 revenue costs over five years (indicative only).

Funding sources include:

- £210,000 Millennium Commission
- The Single Regeneration Budget, BCDC and Centro provide matching funding for the Millennium Commission monies
- Greenways Programme which is sponsored by Telewest (cable company) and the Countryside Commission.

Additional funding could include:

- European monies under the area's Objective 2 status
- Barclays Bank site savers
- BCDC: community business and training grants
- Sandwell MBC: possible community development, environment and recreational grants
- TEC: training activities, particularly where there are links to NVQs and job opportunities
- World Wide Fund for Nature: project grants for habitat enhancement and/or fish survey
- Civic Trust: community projects including habitat preservation and access improvements
- Environment Agency: possible fish restocking
- Urban Life Barclays: environmental enhancement grants
- English Partnerships: site development adjacent to BCDC
- National Urban Forestry Unit: tree planting.

In addition, Groundwork intend to create opportunities for local groups who wish to benefit from Millennium Funds in order to undertake appropriate projects within the programme.

The implementation structure has been developed upon best practice learnt from funded programmes such as City Challenge and the current SRB programme:

Automotive Components Park

- a 'Friends of Ridgeacre' has been set up to aid the development of the Canal Corridor. The group includes local residents, anglers, a police officer, school teacher, conservationists and a member of the Residents Association. The group is affiliated to the British Trust for Conservation Volunteers (BTCV), whose 'skill providers' provide experience in implementing environmental projects alongside interest groups;

- Groundwork Black Country, to be responsible for the development and implementation of a training programme to provide skills to unemployed local people and volunteers;

- a programme manager, to be responsible for monitoring the impact of projects and feeding into the delivery and implementation process;

- users will be encouraged to build maintenance into their activities with potential to extend this within a site-use agreement for user groups;

- local industry will be encouraged to co-operate and become involved in environmental enhancement projects and activities.

LESSONS FOR GOOD PRACTICE

- The provision of a clearly defined *strategy* is important in providing the framework within which individual actions can be developed separately, but in a co-ordinated manner.

- A strategic approach (taken by Groundwork in this case), to address local need which is supported and valued by the local people.

- Here there is local *'ownership'* of the vision, the strategy, paid staff, the projects and the finances, in other words, local management to high professional standards.

- The establishment of a *strong partnership* framework has helped to engender long term commitment and a sense of ownership to reflect the fact that greening and growing are continuous processes and that communities which stand to benefit will likewise evolve and change. The development of a practical, working partnership between the public, private and voluntary sectors is needed to get things done on the ground.

- Groundwork or similar agencies provide the necessary *professional support* and expertise in a way which enables groups to realise their aims - "Professionals on tap and not on top" (John Davidson - Groundwork).

- The development of a system for financial and project management helps to ensure that public and private funds are properly managed.

Contact: Hazel Whittington, Programme Co-ordinator
      Groundwork Black Country, West Midlands House, Gypsy Lane, Willenhall,
      West Midlands, WV13 2HA.

1.2 The Southampton Greenways

INTRODUCTION AND KEY ISSUES

Since the early 1980s, Southampton City Council have been working to establish a network of Greenways in the city. The Greenways are ribbons of open space which follow stream valleys through the city. They form valuable breaks in built-up areas, and in some cases reach out into the open countryside and beyond. They perform a number of important functions in providing areas for recreation, preserving wildlife habitats and enhancing the diversity and quality of Southampton's landscape.

The project provides an example of the positive planning and management of existing wildlife features and the subsequent use of the nature resource for recreation and education.

ACTION TAKEN

Strategy Development

Southampton has an extensive and well established green network of open spaces and woodlands. In order to protect and manage this resource in an efficient and appropriate manner the City Council has in place a policy framework which is based on a thorough assessment and understanding of the wildlife value of the green network.

The development of, and commitment to, the concept of Greenways can be traced back to 1983 when the then Planning and Transportation Committee accepted a report entitled "Linear Open Space Provision". This set out a programme for detailed proposals for linear routes along stream valleys - Greenways. At the time of conception, none of the Greenways was named and, in order to establish a local identity for each site the Council initiated a project with the local community to name each Greenway.

1984 saw the approval of the first land-use policies and strategy for one of the City's Greenways. Further strategies were approved between 1986 and 1995 for six more.

In 1985 the City Council adopted a Greening the City Strategy. This emphasised the City's commitment to protecting and enhancing the natural environment. As part of this, additional money was allocated to the development of the Greenways.

In 1988 the Greenways were used as a pilot to establish a new biological survey and data handling project for the city. The City Council commissioned the Geodata Institute of Southampton University to do the work, which resulted in a report 'Towards a Management Survey of Southampton Greenways'. A computer database was established to store the biological records. Much of this information was later used in the preparation of the City's Nature Conservation Strategy (1992).

In 1992 a 'Members' Panel' was established, as a sub-committee of the City Council's Strategy Development Committee. This provided the focus for Members interested in Greenways and streamlined the reporting and approval procedures for officers.

The Greenways incorporate both City Council and privately owned land. Since their adoption the City Council has continued to develop the Greenways, acquiring privately owned areas when opportunities have arisen.

Design and Implementation

A number of key issues were raised in relation to the design of the Greenways, including:
- *form and function:* the Greenways incorporate a number of different uses and activities (ie nature conservation, informal recreation and active pursuits) which reflect the character of each area. The design response has been to incorporate facilities that reflect these various functions. For example, in areas with important nature conservation features the design response has been suitably low key, incorporating facilities such as paths, boardwalks and fencing to safeguard the nature of the site. In more formal recreational areas, facilities such as children's play grounds are present. One car park has also been provided;
- *minimise impact:* one of the objectives of the project has been to minimise impact within the more sensitive natural environments. This has been achieved in certain parts through the use of boardwalks which pass over wetland habitats causing minimal disturbance, and the planning of

routes to minimise the effect on trees. Contracts include very specific terms aimed at minimising the impact on the environment;

- *natural response*: specification of materials and workmanship has been minimal to ensure a natural response to the environment. Pathways are constructed of compacted hoggin and/or woodchips. Material excavated during pathway construction is retained within the site and allowed to regenerate naturally. Fencing, gates and interpretation markers are all made of wood;

- *interpretation*: interpretation markers and boards are provided throughout the Greenways to give an overall identity, provide an explanation of the importance of certain areas and enable people to follow the routes;

- *recycling*: the reuse of materials has been important in the implementation process for example some of the boardwalks and bridges have been constructed from elm which has had to be removed from other parts of the city as a result of disease;

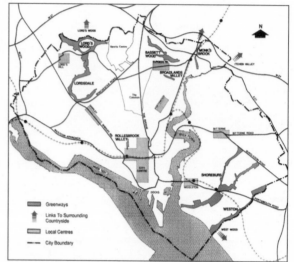

- *safety*: paths are planned to maximise long distance visibility and are kept free of overhanging vegetation;

- *access for all*: disabled access has been made possible in as many parts of the Greenways as is possible.

Community Involvement

Strong links have been forged with the community. In the initial stages, this involvement tended to be informal, with members of the team responding to the needs of a particular group or organisation on an ad hoc basis. The consultation process followed conventional routes in terms of leafleting, exhibitions and public meetings.

The process of consultation today is much more structured. Twelve Community Action Fora have been established across the city comprising representatives from the local community. Community Action managers within the Council provide the point of contact and communication between each forum and the Council, and each forum can set its own agenda of issues. This corporate approach to community consultation is designed to ensure cross departmental working and links between various regeneration programmes.

Provision of board walks and pathways through sensitive woodland environments

Greening the City Grant

Within this framework the City Council has initiated a 'Greening the City Grant' which provides local community groups with a grant up to a maximum of £2,000 to undertake environmental projects including planting, management works, access provision, or for tools to undertake the project.

Greenwatch

This was a trial project run by the City Council to promote a sense of ownership for particular parts of the Greenway once the project had been implemented: it encouraged people to report damage.

Maintenance and Management

CCT has introduced a very structured framework to the maintenance of open areas. However natural environments, as contained within the Greenways, require positive management in order to maintain their diversity and interest. There is no generic specification that can be applied within a CCT contract and there is therefore a need to draw up bespoke management plans for particular areas.

In addition few generalist contractors have been found to possess the skills or equipment required for the necessary specialist work in, for example, a woodland environment.

The net result of these conflicts and difficulties is that officers consider that certain parts of the Greenways should be taken out of CCT and managed in a more responsive and appropriate manner, possibly via the introduction of a ranger service for the Greenways.

PARTNERS

- *City Council:* landowners, strategic planning, contact with local community, technical advice, implementor and manager;
- *Community:* surveys, volunteer time in the design, implementation, management and aftercare of the sites;
- *Private sector:* provision of funds through sponsorship and/or planning gain.

LESSONS FOR GOOD PRACTICE

- Strategic planning and associated planning policy were essential in the establishment of the project and its ability to attract private and public funds.
- The success of the project over time has been greatly assisted by the support of members and of particular individuals.
- Partnership between the Council, members of the community and private sector provided the opportunity to obtain a variety of different skills, labour, equipment and finance.
- Momentum for the project has been maintained by continued publicity, submission of the project for awards, organisation of events and visits from schools and others.
- Multi-disciplinary working provided for informed decision making.
- Effective management needs to be based on scientific information gathered in the field.
- Community grants and initiation have encouraged members of the community to become involved in the implementation and management process.
- Training initiatives in relation to risk assessment and volunteers have allowed the Council to continue to involve members of the community in implementation and aftercare.

Contact: Patrick Baxter Hunter, Group Leader
      Urban Design Services, Southampton City Council, Civic Centre, Southampton , SO14 7LS

1.3 Black Country Urban Forestry Initiative (Woodlands by the Motorway)

INTRODUCTION AND KEY ISSUES

The Black Country Urban Forestry Initiative provides an example of a strategic greening initiative which aims, through the planting of trees and woodlands, to improve the image of a region, to help attract new investment and improve the quality of life for people who live and work in the area. The initiative is led by the Black Country Urban Forestry Unit (1990-95), now the National Urban Forestry Unit (NUFU) and involves local authorities, government agencies, private landowners, voluntary sector agencies and local communities.

To assist in the delivery of the aims and objectives of NUFU, a number of programmes and initiatives have been developed for various parts of the region. In the context of transportation corridors we examine one such programme: Woodlands by the Motorway. The programme focuses on the greening of motorways to enhance image and illustrates NUFU's approach: partnership, community involvement, influencing the practice of others, imaginative use of finance, cost effective woodland establishment and management and maintenance. As the programme is well advanced and supported by well documented technical data on its successes and failures, it provides a useful demonstration model.

Albright and Wilson: tree planting on surplus industrial land (one of the key sites identified by the programme)

ACTION TAKEN

Process

The 'Woodlands by the Motorway' programme, which has been running for four years (1992-96), provides an example of a strategic landscape planning approach to greening in a large, geographically focused area - the M5/M6 transport corridor.

The programme, a partnership between NUFU, the Countryside Commission, Highways Agency and Esso UK plc, provided funding to appoint a dedicated project officer to manage the programme and develop a strategic framework for an area covering 26km^2 of land, along 26km of motorway. Based on visual inspection and examination of background material 225 potential sites (of 0.15ha to 30ha) were identified, for woodland planting and management.

Each site was inspected and assessed using a standard set of criteria in order to determine priorities for action. Criteria used in this assessment included:

- the physical opportunity for planting/improving management;
- the visual quality of the site;
- the visibility of the motorway;
- the local provision of woodland;
- the opportunities for linking/clustering sites;
- the likely opportunities for finance or for achieving improvement.

Using the above criteria, approximately 100 sites were assessed as high priority for tree and woodland planting or management. There was a further stage of sifting of the priority sites to establish a strategy of action for the early phase of the project. A decision was made to concentrate initially on certain natural groupings of linked or clustered sites. The benefits of concentrating on these 'target areas' were seen as:

- achieving economies of scale in implementation;
- networking and sustaining local interest;
- maximising impact in terms of creating significant and discernible improvements.

Thirteen target areas were identified, comprising 45 different sites.

Individual projects were developed for each of the 45 sites in consultation with all relevant parties (landowners, local authorities, other agencies and the community), in response to the particular physical circumstances and uses of each site. Examples include:

- *Delves Green:* a large tree planting programme on a large underused open space located within a residential area of South Walsall;
- *Pleck Park:* the introduction of woodland into a conventional public park;
- *Albright and Wilson Chemical Works:* the introduction of woodland planting onto industrial sites.

Tree planting along the motorway

Community consultation

Community consultation is seen as an essential pre-requisite of any project. At the neighbourhood level, community involvement on individual sites has ranged from simple leaflet production to Planning for Real exercises. Although time consuming and costly, NUFU have found Planning for Real to be extremely useful in neighbourhoods with significant areas of open space where there has been a history of vandalism.

A Planning for Real exercise was undertaken at Delves Green where the scale of the consultation was very large. The Residents' Association helped to make a model of the Green which was displayed in libraries near the site. Over 3,000 local households were circulated with details of the venues. Local people put forward ideas for the future of the Green in a comments book and a steering group of local residents worked with NUFU to formulate a design. This was agreed with the majority of residents, then worked up into a woodland planting scheme by NUFU.

In addition many of the projects seek to involve the community either in the actual planting or in projects associated with woodland and/or the use of wood. The Pleck Park project incorporated a community arts project involving teenage groups in using wood materials.

The approach to implementation of woodland planting adopted by NUFU is one of low cost/high performance. The scale of the projects is often substantial and there is a need to employ cost-effective techniques which encourage minimal maintenance. The approach adopted by NUFU is to speed up the process of natural regeneration by planting native pioneer species, a combination of forestry techniques and a naturalistic approach. NUFU has been able to demonstrate through research that its methods are cheaper than other, more intensive, planting methods. At Pleck Park, NUFU were able to demonstrate to the Department of Leisure at Sandwell MBC that, through the use of various grant regimes, introducing trees into the park would not result in any additional capital expenditure and would in fact lead to a reduction in maintenance costs.

Indigenous tree planting mixed with wild flowers provide low cost alternative on derelict land

Implementation

Wherever possible, implementation is carried out by approved forestry contractors. NUFU or the Forestry Commission supervise contracts for any schemes funded by the Highway Agency. Maintenance contracts run for three years. Long term management guidelines are prepared for site owners prior to the three year establishment period ending.

Revenue generation

In association with Groundwork Black Country, NUFU is looking at the potential for generating income from the woodland by creating a local market for the sale of timber products and hence make woodland production a self sustaining activity.

The project is in its early stages. Groundwork is currently looking at the potential of timber stations and the development of community based management initiatives to take the process forward.

FUNDING AND PARTNERS

The project has been running for three years and has cost £40,000 per annum to run and manage, funded by the Highways Agency, the Countryside Commission and Esso in partnership.

Capital investment of between £80,000 to £100,000 per annum splits into two broad types:

- 100% funding by the Highways Agency as part of its off-site planting programme (50% of schemes);
- those funded by 'tailor made' packages using funding from a variety of different sources including the European Regional Development Fund, English Partnerships, The Forestry Authority (Woodland Grant Scheme and Woodland Community Supplement), Black Country Development Corporation, Environment Agency, local authorities and private landowners.

KEY LESSONS FOR GOOD PRACTICE

- The development of an overall strategy helped to focus attention upon a recognisable programme which potential partners could understand and identify with and provided a framework within which projects could be developed.

Thinning of trees to allow views into and out of woodland to increase the feeling of security

- The process of community involvement has provided a number of key lessons:
  - consultation should be held within the community itself and if possible should be related to a particular activity or event;
  - people should be kept informed. Leaflet distribution proved to be effective. The format adopted by NUFU is simple and consistent;
  - consistent involvement of individuals who should retain a strong presence in the area;
  - more generalised consultation should be followed up by one to one discussion with those people directly affected by the planting;
  - modest planting projects often provide the catalyst to encourage more substantial community involvement;
  - involvement helps to reduce vandalism.
- Research undertaken for NUFU by Land Use Consultants (1995) has demonstrated that:
  - informal woodlands (naturally colonising and pioneer style) with provision for casual public access can be considerably cheaper to manage than grassland;
  - where there is a greater degree of public access, and a tidier woodland is required (woodland in public parks), maintenance costs increase, but still compare favourably with those for rough grasslands and meadows;
  - about half of the cost of urban woodland maintenance is tree-related: the other half is accounted for by path and signboard maintenance, litter collection and wardening;
  - smaller grassland sites are proportionately more expensive to maintain.
- Implementation should be carried out by approved forestry contractors who possess appropriate skills to undertake the work.
- The development of detailed monitoring indicators relevant to greening:
  - value for money; capital and life cycle cost of different types of greening;
  - biodiversity indicators: currently being developed by NUFU in relation mainly to gardens on numbers and types of species and habitat variety;
  - community involvement: number of meetings and numbers of people consulted;

Tree planting on derelict land adjacent to school

- reduction in vandalism: the number of incidents of vandalism;
- atmospheric pollution: the reduction of ambient levels of gaseous and particulate pollution;
- timber output increment: turnover from woodland planting/production.

Contact: Nerys Jones, NUFU, The Science Park, Wolverhampton, WV9

1.4 Royate Hill Local Nature Reserve

INTRODUCTION AND KEY ISSUES

In 1989, British Rail moved to sell a linear strip of open land next to a railway viaduct at Royate Hill, Bristol for residential development. The community which surrounded the site had other ideas. Although the site had not been touched by British Rail for many years, the community had used it for informal recreation purposes, and it performed an important local amenity function which they were not prepared to relinquish.

It has been selected for this good practice guide, not as an example of particularly innovative design but rather because it provides an example of collective community involvement to prevent an important amenity resource being lost to development. The community now manage the site for recreation and nature conservation.

The project is also of interest because it is maintained by the community at a relatively low cost, using funding and resources from a variety of different sources.

ACTION TAKEN

Process

A disused linear strip of land lying next to a railway viaduct and surrounded by fairly high density residential development has, since 1965, performed an important amenity function. It is a focus for local community activity and supports a number of different uses and functions including an orchard, vegetable garden, informal recreation and local community events.

The local plan recognised the nature conservation value of the site, but the then owners of the site, British Rail, decided to sell the site for development. In 1989 a consortium of developers purchased the land at residential value. The developers were told by the local authority that they would not receive planning permission, but planning applications were submitted, and appeals were subsequently submitted to the Secretary of State for the Environment against non-determination of the applications. The appeals were refused. The site, however, remained in the hands of the developers and access was restricted. In 1992 the developers returned to the site with bulldozers to clear rubbish which had been illegally flytipped. The work was undertaken insensitively and police and planning officers were called. An injunction was placed on the site preventing any further work.

These actions by the developers led Avon County Council to put together a case to acquire the land compulsorily. A second inquiry took place, led by Avon County Council with joint support from residents and the Avon County Wildlife Trust.

The approach taken by the residents was, in their words, "highly emotive". The importance of the land to the community and the levels of use made of it were emphasised, together with the wildlife value of the site which was measured and scientifically recorded. In April 1995, Avon County Council was given permission to acquire the site and took possession in January 1996 although the precise valuation of the site remains unresolved. This is the first time a Compulsory Purchase Order (CPO) has been used to acquire land declared as a Local Nature Reserve.

Community Participation

The strength of involvement and the continued momentum that has been generated since the site was threatened by development in 1989, together with the location of the site at the heart of the residential community, has meant that feelings about the site are very strong. The networks of communication have become well established. There are key representatives within each part of the community surrounding the site and this, together with the cross links between groups and local business, means that any issue can be dealt with quickly.

It is hoped that, as school groups become involved, the lessons learnt can be transferred to the next generation and the current volunteers will be able to step back for others to take over their role.

Design, Implementation and Maintenance

The injunctions placed upon the developers were modified following the granting of the CPO, so that work could be carried out by the community on the site, provided that it was fully documented and in accordance with a management plan (prepared by the Urban Wildlife Trust in consultation with local residents).

The initial stages of work involved the residents in reconstruction of walls and fences and the provision of proper access points and paths. Rubbish has been cleared and trees planted. The approach has been to gradually upgrade the site as money is available and in accordance with the management plan. Schools and other local groups use the site and are involved in the site's maintenance and regeneration.

Maintenance of the site is undertaken by a core group of 15-20 volunteers. Members of the community have attended courses funded by the Wildlife Trust on various topics including risk assessment.

The precise arrangement between the local authority and the residents is still to be clarified. This has been complicated by the demise of Avon County Council. The new committee structure is still being established. It is proposed, however, that the site will be handed over to the Wildlife Trust to manage.

FUNDING AND PARTNERS

Before the local resident groups had any legitimate control of the site they could not qualify for any grant assistance, although the World Wildlife Trust donated £500 towards the cost of producing of proofs of evidence for the CPO inquiry. They also received an Age Resource Grant from the Prince's Trust for £1,000 and other donations were raised within the community via the staging of various fund raising events, publicity, business sponsorship and donations (including finance, labour, tools/products).

Now that the site has been declared a Local Nature Reserve, grants can be applied for. So far money has been received from:

- *Barclays Bank*; for boundary fencing
- *Avon County Council*; £4,000 (boundary wall)
- *British Gas*; £1,000
- *Wessex Water*; £500 (for cleaning the brook)
- *Environmental Improvement Grant (Avon County Council)*; £700.

A trust fund set up in 1993, managed by the Wildlife Trust, provides the mechanism to control funding.

OUTCOME

The Nature Reserve now provides an important amenity resource and has effectively utilised a derelict and underused piece of surplus land. It offers recreational and educational experience for all ages and provides a model for community resilience and resourcefulness.

LESSONS FOR GOOD PRACTICE

- Perhaps the biggest lesson to be learnt is how developers approach development. Development and the conservation of wildlife should be treated as compatible actions. Developers should be encouraged to be sensitive to what they are building into and to take on board the issues of diversity, natural habitat creation, access, drainage, the provision of open spaces and their long term management and maintenance and impact upon the wider environmental context.

Contact: Sophia Price, Conservation Officer, Leisure Services Directorate
Colston House, Colston Street, Bristol, BS1 5AQ

1.5 Leicester Riverside

INTRODUCTION AND KEY ISSUES

The Leicester Riverside project is focused on the River Soar, which runs from north to south through the centre of the city. It is one of the city's most important wildlife arteries, connecting the city with the countryside and it supports a wide variety of habitats, functions and activities. The local authority have recognised the importance of the riverside for some time and channelled resources into the regeneration of the area to maximise the river's environmental and recreational potential.

The riverside provides for a variety of recreational needs

It provides an excellent example of the translation of strategic policy into projects and initiatives on the ground.

ACTION TAKEN

Strategic Framework

The strategic framework for the Riverside area is provided by the following:

Habitat Survey: a detailed and comprehensive ecological survey of open space areas in Leicester undertaken by the City Wildlife Project (part of the Leicestershire and Rutland Trust for Nature Conservation) between 1983 and 1987. The survey provided information on the distribution of wildlife and habitat type, identified key sites and corridors, and important links of high conservation value together with those of limited value. This base line data was used to prepare the Leicester Ecology Strategy.

Leicester Ecology Strategy: provides a framework for nature conservation aimed at:

- the enhancement, protection and sensitive management of the ecological, recreational, educational and visual quality of open spaces;
- the provision of a network of natural green spaces with improved access to the countryside;
- improving the quality of life for residents of the city.

Leicester City Local Plan: ecology policies, aims and implementation. The themes developed in the ecology strategy have been absorbed into the statutory plan, and fall into four main policy areas:

- *Nature conservation and development:*
  - designating site alert maps;
  - protecting areas of greatest ecological importance through the designation of Local Nature Reserves;
  - purchasing sites of ecological importance;
  - drawing up appropriate management plans for implementation;
  - resisting change of use from open space;
  - designating a green network of wedges, corridors and other areas and features;
  - safeguarding floodable areas;
  - consulting neighbouring authorities to protect strategic green wedges;
  - requiring developers to submit details showing impacts of development on the ecological interest of sites or features, and any mitigation measures;
  - devising guidance for approved development which identifies features of wildlife or landscape interest to be retained in the scheme, specifying measures to restore or compensate for the loss of wildlife habitats and specifying landscape requirements;
  - using conditions and agreements on planning consents to enhance the wildlife interest.
- *Managing and improving habitats for wildlife:*
  - organising training courses for employees involved in management;
  - establishing a system of advice on nature conservation and promoting model examples of working practices;

- promoting nature conservation in designing and implementing environmental schemes;
- adopting management practices which conserve and increase the opportunities for wildlife;
- liaising with other major public and private landowners and encouraging land management practices which are sympathetic to the needs of wildlife;
- enhancing the ecological value of open space, and public open space;
- giving high priority to low cost natural schemes;
- identifying opportunities for the improvement or development of wildlife habitats through changes in management and the creation of new habitats;
- improving and enhancing water and air quality;
- planting native species.

• *Promoting the enjoyment and understanding of nature:*
- seeking views and involving local people in the planning, management and implementation of schemes;
- providing access to areas of wildlife interest and encouraging greater use and understanding;
- promoting awareness and understanding through the provision of way-marked nature trails, leaflets, exhibitions, videos and nature centres.

• *Monitoring and Review:*
- updating the Leicester Habitat Survey;
- monitoring the success of each individual scheme;
- monitoring public involvement;
- preparing an annual report.

Local Action

The Leicester Riverside is one of the City's strategic green wedges which was recognised by the ecology strategy as being of significant value. It comprises a number of different land uses and supports a range of different habitats and landscapes. The river provided the link between a number of important open spaces including Abney Park (a formal public park), Aylestone Meadows (an important ecological area) and Church Gardens (a small historic city park). The importance of the riverside has been recognised for some time, in terms of tourism, recreation and ecology. For these reasons significant and consistent resources have been assigned to the project, allowing for a number of projects to be developed along the riverside including Aylestone Meadows, which was a former tip site now reclaimed as a nature reserve. More recently the project has enjoyed a more co-ordinated approach to its planning and development. The Countryside Commission part funded the appointment of a Riverside Project Officer two years ago. The Officer, who is an ecologist by training, is charged with co-ordinating the activities of the City Council on the ground in delivering individual projects, responding to particular issues and promoting community involvement in the process. She is supported by two rangers.

Approach

Due to the mixed ownership pattern within the river corridor, implementation has progressed on a more ad hoc basis than some of the other case studies: progress has been made as opportunities have arisen or finance made available, or as a result of private sector/community interest. The appointment of a dedicated project officer, however, has enabled the Council to be more proactive in encouraging projects and activities.

The provision for a continuous pathway along the riverside

Community Involvement

Community involvement has been a key element in realising projects and has proved to be a useful catalyst in achieving success. Along the riverside, safety issues and fear of crime have had to be addressed involving close liaison with the police. A 'Friends of the Riverside' scheme has been established and various projects have been developed, including the launch of a 'Green Life Boat' to promote river cleaning. British Waterways lent the boat for a trial period and the community and schools assisted in the clean up operation on a voluntary basis. The local paper supported the project by launching a "green life" page. It is now a regular feature.

Maintenance and Management

The riverside area is maintained under two contract areas administered by a client group within the Council's Leisure Service Department. The contract is administered across the authority which makes it hard to respond to site specific issues. However there is a management plan targeting specific management techniques for natural areas.

An ecology officer works alongside the contracts officer to develop an integrated management/maintenance approach. However, it is felt that there is a need for a dedicated management team to deal with the different aspects of the riverside: at present a number of different departments/organisations deal with different parts of the riverside. There is also a need for site specific training for contractors, which takes an overview rather than a subject based approach.

FUNDING AND PARTNERS

Funding sources have included the Urban Programme, City Challenge, British Waterways, The Environment Agency (bridges and canal structures) and the City Council. Strong political support and consistent financial commitment have been important to the success of the project. In the future Leicester City Council intend to be far more active in encouraging riverside landowners to contribute to its upkeep and improvement. A number of organisations are starting to participate in the process and have contributed, either financially or in kind, by undertaking works in consultation with the project officer.

LESSONS FOR GOOD PRACTICE

- The appointment of a dedicated project officer has allowed the City Council to be more proactive and responsive in initiating, developing and implementing projects on the ground.
- The provision of a policy framework which is supported by survey information allows for consistent decision making, appropriate protection and management of resources and consistency over time.
- The diversity of landscapes supported by an environment such as the Leicester Riverside needs customised management and maintenance.
- Dedicated management teams with appropriate skills should deal with the different aspects of a project of this scale and complexity.
- A riverside or similar environment can be used as the stimulus and focus for involvement and can encourage interaction between many different parts of the community.

Contact: Paul Leonard Williams, Leicester City Council
New Walk Centre, Welford Road, Leicester, LE1 6ZG

2.1 Neighbourhood Nature

INTRODUCTION AND KEY ISSUES

Neighbourhood Nature is one of a number of special programmes being led by the National Urban Forestry Unit (see Case Study 1.3 for an explanation of the background to NUFU) in partnership with the Urban Wildlife Trust (one of 46 UK Country Wildlife Trusts) and Walsall City Challenge.

Site preparation

The project operates within a defined area of Walsall (470ha) and is concerned with raising community awareness about urban trees, woodland and wildlife.

In relation to the greening of residential areas this case study looks at the work undertaken on a housing estate where a number of Neighbourhood Nature projects have been successfully implemented.

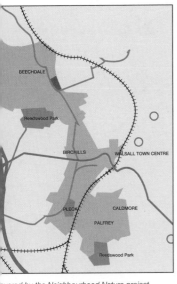
...overed by the Neighbourhood Nature project

ACTION TAKEN

Strategy, design and implementation

A project officer employed by NUFU and the Urban Wildlife Trust (UWT) is responsible for the delivery of the project and for raising awareness about urban forestry and woodland wildlife with members of the local community.

One of the areas where the project has been initiated is the Beechdale Estate, a high density, primarily council owned housing area dating from the 1950s. Gardens are small and public spaces comprise grassed areas with limited tree cover. Under the programme a series of projects have been developed including:

Green Trees Scheme: the streets within the estate offered limited opportunities for tree planting. It was therefore decided that front gardens should provide the focus for a campaign of planting to demonstrate how a housing estate could present a green image despite insufficient room for street trees. A campaign was launched offering residents the opportunity to apply for a free tree. Leaflets distributed to all households encouraged residents to choose their tree from a range of pioneer species selected by Neighbourhood Nature. Orders were taken by the project officer and trees were delivered and planted by schoolchildren.

Further leaflets advised participants how to care for the trees. Each tree was issued with a mulch mat which reduced weeds in the establishment years.

Beechdale Corner Plots: many open spaces had potential for planting. A survey identified some 60 plots as suitable for tree planting - no interference from overhead or underground cables, buildings, suitable size and high visibility. From these, six sites were selected as suitable pilots due to their prominent position. All residents whose homes overlooked the sites were consulted in a door-to-door survey which used plans of the proposed planting and an artist's impression of how the plot would look after twenty years. The results of the consultation were displayed in the neighbourhood office and were taken forward for planting.

Young trees (60-90cms) were planted at two metre spacings, and thorny shrubs and hedges planted alongside garden walls in response to concerns about security. Large species such as oak, ash and beech were planted in positions at appropriate distances from buildings, using woodchip mulch to control weeds.

School children planting

Contractors were appointed to plant and maintain the plots for three years. Local residents and groups of school children assisted with the planting and any plants lost will be replaced annually as part of the contract.

A second phase of garden tree and corner plot schemes has been implemented on the estate. Residents have nominated sites which have been co-ordinated by the project officer to follow corridors through the estate and link with external wildlife corridors.

Garden Birds Survey: residents are encouraged to undertake a survey of bird species as part of a measurement of biodiversity.

Post planting, whip with wood chip mulch

Community Involvement

Community involvement has been central to the project. The project officer has identified a number of key procedures and activities which have ensured the success of the project including:

- *consistency of involvement:* the single and continued presence of the project officer has enabled the community to start to identify her as the 'Tree Woman' and has engendered a sense of trust and encouraged further involvement;

- *consistency of communication:* all leaflets and publications circulated as part of the projects have followed a consistent format and style;

- *keeping the community informed:* every action and outcome from meetings has been reported back to the community, and a contact name provided so enquiries can be answered;

- *ensuring local context:* all meetings are held at a local venue which is already well used by the community. In addition, it has been found useful to associate the consultation with a well established local event;

- *provision of information:* the use of visual material to illustrate how a particular scheme will look proved a useful tool in engaging the community and obtaining reaction;

- *making relevant:* not all residents were interested in tree planting and the project officer found it difficult to generate interest using conventional methods, resorting instead to alternative methods, including identifying what particular groups did with their free time. For example, an Asian women's group, involved with garment production was encouraged to transfer these skills to the production of 'flags' and 'banners' to 'dress' trees. A tree dressing festival was run in association with the project;

- *keeping focused:* consulting those residents directly affected by a particular scheme;

- *quick successes:* the implementation of preliminary projects helps to initiate and sustain interest and enthusiasm;

- *flexibility:* being prepared to alter and respond to different ideas;

- *project champions:* attempting to identify core groups of locals to help organise events and disseminate information.

Resident aftercare

FUNDING AND PARTNERS

While the basic costs of running the Neighbourhood Nature programme are covered by Walsall City Challenge, there are insufficient funds to cover management time invested by NUFU and UWT. Individual projects are funded from a range of sources including the Forestry Authority, private sponsors and grant making trusts.

The partners in the project are:

- *NUFU:* seconds a project officer to the project, and provides technical and landscape design support and publicity.

- *Urban Wildlife Trust:* provides technical and landscape design support.

- *Walsall City Challenge:* provides funding for the project.

OUTCOMES

- The programme which is relatively cheap and simple to implement has proved successful in engaging the community, and there is a general consensus among residents that the trees improve the visual quality of the estate.
- Levels of vandalism have declined through subsequent phases of the project's development.
- The project has stimulated active involvement at schools and has initiated a number of educational projects and programmes.

LESSONS FOR GOOD PRACTICE

- The Neighbourhood Nature project is one of a number of initiatives being promoted on the Beechdale Estate which combine to tackle physical, social and environmental problems. Planting trees under the programme, has provided the impetus for further action in initiating and encouraging effective community involvement.

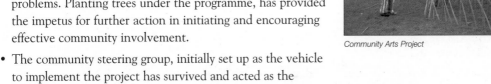

Community Arts Project

- The community steering group, initially set up as the vehicle to implement the project has survived and acted as the stimulus for continued involvement in other, longer term projects on the estate.
- The planting techniques used have been cheaper to maintain than mown grass areas.
- The project has developed a range of indicators to monitor environmental projects including take up of training, number of schools and members of the community involved in the project, grant take up, grant leverage and numbers of events.
- Effective community involvement requires consistency of involvement, communication and information to be relevant to the community, flexibility, the generation of quick successes and the identification of project champions to help organise events and the dissemination of information.

Contact: Nerys Jones, NUFU, The Science Park, Wolverhampton, WV9

2.2 Kings Cross Estate Action

INTRODUCTION AND KEY ISSUES

Bramber Green and two historic London squares (Argyle and Regent) form part of the open space network within a residential estate in Kings Cross, London. A combination of misuse and inadequate and inappropriate management had led to decline and problems associated with drug abuse, street drinking, dogs and fly tipping. The residential population surrounding the squares had abandoned these spaces and despite their location at the heart of the residential estate they no longer performed the amenity function for which they had originally been designed.

Regent Square before improvements

The problems experienced in the open spaces had also spread to the public areas of the surrounding blocks of flats. The residents lobbied the London Borough of Camden to rehabilitate the estate. This led to a successful bid under the Estate Action Programme for £46 million. The project is currently being implemented and as part of the process the open spaces have been upgraded and improved in close collaboration with the resident community.

In relation to the Greening the City initiative this case study provides an example of how a 'green' resource which has ceased to serve the local community as a result of misuse and mismanagement can, through comprehensive action and resident involvement, be transformed into a positive asset which is relevant to the needs of the existing community.

The masterplan for the whole estate

ACTION TAKEN

Strategy Formulation

An extensive public consultation programme was initiated in 1993. A 'twin-track' approach was developed: area wide, through a Community Steering Group; and at a local level, within nine 'localities' identified through a Planning for Real exercise.

Crime and fear of crime were raised as the key issues of concern to residents in relation to buildings and the open spaces. More specifically for the open space, the consultation exercise highlighted the need for:

- better maintenance of green spaces;
- enforcement of bylaws;
- closure at night;
- community park rangers;
- wheelchair access;
- further local consultation.

In parallel with the consultation the design teams undertook their own survey of the buildings and the open spaces. The results formed the basis for an overall plan for the area, which identified key schemes and themes for the public realm, open spaces and buildings. The community were consulted on the strategy and amendments made. Based on this strategy a bid was put forward for Estates Action funding.

Design and Implementation

For the open spaces, the key objective was to use design and management to break the cycle of decline and misuse in the open space areas.

Argyle and Regent Squares were originally designed in the late 19th Century along traditional lines, responding simply in terms of shape, pathways, tree planting and boundary treatment. This basic structure was still in evidence, although suffering from erosion and misuse.

The designers recognised the potential for the squares to develop different characteristics, with each making its own unique contribution to the neighbourhood:

- Regent Square: historic/traditional - quiet sitting area;
- Argyle Square: contemporary/urban - mixed activities;
- Bramber Green: community based/habitat rich.

The approach has been to provide simply detailed spaces which are easy to maintain and with visibility into and within the spaces. Features such as serpentine paths, and the detailing of railing make historic references, while dog grids, electronic locks and use of materials such as resin bound gravel for surfaces, provide modern design solutions to assist in the management and maintenance of spaces.

Reuse of Materials

A key element in the process has been to work with the existing structure and retain as much of the existing material and mature tree planting as possible, including the reuse of York stone paving, railings and top soil.

Public Art

An arts programme, 'Making Visible', is being run within the estate. A local artist has been commissioned to develop a scheme to link the distinctly different spaces of Bramber Green, Regent Square and Sidmouth Mews. It is envisaged that this will take the form of a planting scheme involving local schoolchildren.

Community Involvement

As with the initial bid, community involvement in the design and implementation process was considered essential for success. The simple structure adopted by the designers allowed for the accommodation of a range of uses and functions. An interactive process was adopted involving the designers presenting ideas and the community responding. Thus the outcome was comprehensively informed by the needs of the residents and users of the spaces.

Specific issues raised included:

Security: the approach adopted for open spaces involved a clearer definition of private space and the encouragement of a feeling of ownership and responsibility for communal spaces. Measures included:

Regent Square after; removal of rubbish, provision of new railings; paths following desire lines, provision of new seating and perimeter planting

- concentrating pedestrian movement through the estates;
- removing extensive shrub planting and their replacement with lower more transparent shrubs;
- improved lighting;
- new fences and gates to be locked at night;
- introducing a warden to patrol the public spaces.

The crime prevention officer and the police were involved from the earliest stages of the design process.

Dogs: an emotive issue resolved by an overall strategy for the three spaces which defined dog walking and dog free areas.

Play activities: Argyle Square incorporates a kick about area and a small playground, designed in consultation with local schoolchildren who have also been involved in the planting process.

Planting: selection of plants and materials was undertaken in consultation with the local community. Evergreen and hardy varieties were selected.

Management and Maintenance

The maintenance contracts have been specifically tailored to the requirements of the particular open spaces. These replace the generalised contracts aimed at reducing maintenance costs through a less intensive maintenance regime involving reduced mowing and weeding, simple and cheap materials.

Training

Contractors employed local trainees during implementation under a training programme aimed at local youngsters and the long-term unemployed, to help them gain construction and trade skill qualifications.

During each year of the five year programmes, 30 people will attend training courses organised by Camden Training Centre, and funded by Camden Council, working towards National Vocational Qualifications in horticulture, painting and decorating and carpentry.

PARTNERS

There has been a close working relationship between:

- *The London Borough of Camden:* project management, planning and statutory approvals, technical advisors and maintenance.
- *The community:* key involvement in decision making process.
- *Consultants:* facilitators of the design process with the community, liaison between different partners and responsible for design and implementation.

LESSONS FOR GOOD PRACTICE

- Design for an intensively used area should be driven by management and function of spaces rather than aesthetics.
- Each element of the scheme was designed in consultation with the residents, the ultimate users, creating a sense of ownership of the open spaces.
- Safety and security were crucial. These were achieved by increasing visibility through the removal of dense planting and structures; the simple definition of spaces in terms of form and function/public or private; increasing the intensity of use of certain key routes; and the use of lighting and CCTV. The most significant element for the residents, however, involved the introduction of a warden to patrol the spaces.
- The designers worked with current health and safety legislation to produce a design which is relevant to, and reflected the needs of, the community, rather than producing sterile play areas which remain unused and eventually vandalised.

The project team and community representatives

- The re-design of the open spaces has led to a new tailor-made maintenance contract, the aim of which is to make it relevant and cost effective by using more robust hard and soft materials.
- The simplicity of the current design and robustness of the original historic design framework will make future intervention and adaptation easy to achieve. This is considered essential in places such as Kings Cross where there is a large and ever changing population.
- The re-opening of the open spaces has been accompanied by a series of events, thus encouraging people back into the spaces and making them part of the community.

Contact: Des Dally, Tibbalds Monro
    31 Earl Street, London, EC2A 2HR

2.3 Springfield Community Garden, Bradford

INTRODUCTION AND KEY ISSUES

The Holmewood Council estate in Bradford has been the subject of a major Estate Action Project linked with a City Challenge project. Local residents were concerned that most people living on the estate were not familiar with gardening and possessed limited knowledge of environmental issues, food production and cookery. The Springfield Garden aims to rectify these shortcomings.

ACTION TAKEN

These considerations led to proposals to develop the Springfield Garden on a 7.5 hectare site on the edge of the Holmewood estate. Holmewood is a peripheral estate on the edge of the green belt and was part of a council owned farm. The site is now being developed as a sustainable horticulture centre and has been designed using the principles of permaculture. It is the first publicly funded project in the UK to be based on permaculture principles. Permaculture is, according to its developer, *"a system of assembling conceptual, material and strategic components in a pattern which functions to benefit life in all its forms"*.

Springfield project centre

Although this seems highly theoretical, in practice it is enabling the designers of Springfield Garden to produce an area which is capable of meeting many of the basic needs not normally well provided for in a western urban habitat.

The main functions of Springfield Garden are:

- to grow foodstuffs;
- to provide training opportunities for the unemployed and people with learning difficulties;
- to assist local people with information and practical help with the design and maintenance of gardens;
- to provide plants and materials to local gardeners;
- to provide food processing and home economics facilities;
- to provide safe recreation and playing space for young users of the site;
- to provide workshop space for green woodworking (ie green wood from pollarding).

Within the site a new timber building is being created which will have two main sections. The first will be a large community potting shed and workshop. The second will be a communal kitchen facility which will also function as the office for the project. The two units are joined by a toilet block which will recycle all waste into a compost.

Community Involvement

The project has been community led from the beginning. Indeed, this is a community development project specialising in environmental matters, rather than an environmental project which specialises in community matters. The community involvement has led to the provision of:

- allotments (standard and organic);
- non-digging vegetarian gardening experimentation;
- small formal gardens;
- three types of pond (ranging from ornamental to ditch);
- rough play area;
- polythene growing tunnels heated by hot boxes (decomposing compost);
- cash crop growing areas;
- mulch production area;
- willow production area;
- sculpture area (incorporating a pagan temple).

Springfield project site

The project is providing training opportunities for:

- a school for children with learning difficulties and behavioural problems;
- adults with severe learning difficulties;
- care in the community residents via local voluntary groups;
- a local college needing placements for BTEC courses in Amenity Horticulture;
- the local community with help and advice being given on gardening, food production, home economics matters and care of fauna.

Springfield and nearby estate

Local residents of all ages drop into the project as they wish rather than take part in structured activities. This 'drop-in' function will be increased when the new timber building is opened. Specific projects have been designed so that children can make a contribution to the scheme, particularly during the summer holidays.

Consideration is now being given to ways of improving local decision making to encourage the maximum take up of opportunity and involvement by site users. The formal decision making process is via a sub-committee of the Local Agenda 21 group.

FUNDING AND PARTNERS

The principal source of financial support for the project has been the City Challenge, and discussion is now taking place with the local authority to ensure that the funding requirements continue to be met, as part of City Challenge's forward strategy. Other sources of funding and partners have been:

- *Bradford City Council:* an important source of finance and support. The project reports to a sub-committee of the Council, and the lead officer who developed the project is based within the Chief Executive's policy unit.

- *Bradford City Challenge:* the original developer of the project, City Challenge provided funds to buy out the lease of the fields, and for renovation and maintenance.

Springfield garden beds

- *The local community:* members of the community suggested the basis for the project, provided volunteers to work on it, use its facilities, take its ideas out into the wider community and are involved in the direction of it.

The total cost of running the project is about £70,000 a year with income from grants, sale of services and sale of produce.

OUTCOMES

- 7.5 hectares of land brought into productive use (previously used for rough grazing);
- over 700 trees planted;
- over 300 local residents undertaking regular activity on the estate;
- over 25 training opportunities created for a variety of local needs groups.

Other outcomes are harder to define:

- increased knowledge of horticulture;
- gardens brought back into use;
- locally grown produce;
- improved health of participants because of exercise and diet;
- reduction in vandalism because of youth involvement;
- improved local self-esteem and confidence.

LESSONS FOR GOOD PRACTICE

- Siting is all important for a project such as this. If a large site had existed in the middle of the estate it would not have been suitable as some aspects of the project might seem rather rough or scruffy. Adjacent to the site are large stretches of unimaginatively and expensively maintained, Council owned green space, which could be developed much more attractively and productively using bio diverse methodologies.

- Many residents of depressed, rundown areas have been 'turned off' participating in society generally. They need a 'key' to turn them on again. Some can be turned on by sport, others by the arts, and others by music. Springfield Garden is showing that some can be turned on by participation in environmental matters.

- The organisers have deliberately kept this as a largely non-qualification project. No one is forced onto NVQ programmes. This is clearly important if long term unemployed people and other people who have 'withdrawn' from society are to be involved. But there are possibilities for the creation of community businesses and more formal qualification activities as the project establishes itself more and perhaps works on an expanded site.

- The perma-culture concept is one that is clearly understood in cities in the third world with much productive use of land in and adjacent to urban areas. It is, however, not a concept widely used in Europe. The idea of using waste materials in a virtuous productive cycle within an urban area to create food and avoiding the two way transportation of materials is one that could be explored more closely.

- Getting the right staff is vital for a project of this type. Most of the work of the staff is with people rather than horticulture. In many ways the horticulture on this project is a means to an end of working with people suffering from a variety of problems and young users of the site.

Contact: David Melling, Chief Executive's Office, Bradford City Council
      Room 145, City Hall, Bradford, BD1 1HY

3.1 Bedfont Lakes

INTRODUCTION AND KEY ISSUES

Bedfont Lakes Country Park, located within the London Borough of Hounslow, West London provides an example of a large scale land reclamation project funded largely by the private sector.

The site provides an innovative example of a local authority and private developer working together to bring a large tract of despoiled green belt land back into use as a Country Park, providing for nature conservation and recreation for the local and wider population.

ACTION TAKEN

Strategy Development

In 1987, the site, now referred to as Bedfont Lakes, comprised 100 hectares of former gravel workings which had been largely infilled. The site formed a fragmented pocket of open land within an otherwise densely populated environment. The quality of the landscape was poor, as a result of minimal reclamation, and it suffered from problems associated with flytipping, the presence of non-conforming uses and vandalism. As a result the site remained largely unused despite the presence of a large residential population nearby.

New landscapes combine with existing trees to create attractive nature conservation area

The then Greater London Development Plan included the site within the green belt. However, the London Borough of Hounslow recognised that apart from separating residential communities, the site failed to fulfil any of the other positive functions of green belt and that what was needed was a more positive approach to the site to secure its long term open space function. An opportunity was created to modify the boundary of the green belt through the production of a new plan for the area: the West Area Local Plan. In 1987 the majority owner of the site (Rutland Hall) was invited to work up proposals for a comprehensive scheme.

The initial scheme incorporated about 20 hectares of commercial, residential and industrial development, 75 hectares of land which would remain as green belt and which would either be laid out for recreation or be retained/enhanced for nature conservation purposes, and the remainder, a refurbished cemetery.

The basis of this comprehensive approach was that sufficient land would be released from the green belt to provide for development capable of generating funds to pay for the necessary infrastructure, the creation of a country park and its continued maintenance.

The local residents were consulted on the scheme and it was incorporated by the London Borough of Hounslow into their West Area Local Plan. The inspector at the Local Plan Inquiry accepted the approach adopted by the local authority as an exceptional case. As a result, Rutland Hall submitted an outline planning application for the scheme and a proposed earthworks proposal. Detailed applications followed and the scheme was implemented in accordance with a phasing plan, incorporated within a planning agreement (made under Section 52 of the Town and Country Planning Act 1970) for the site.

Pathway through new heathland landscape

Design

The layout of the open space areas was derived from two basic environmental and planning objectives. In the first place it was intended to conserve and enhance areas of the site which had a high nature conservation and/or landscape value and to make areas which lent themselves to recreational use accessible to the public or, alternatively, prepare them for use by particular recreation interests (for example fishing, horse riding or motorcycling). The second objective involved the redefinition of the boundary of the green belt in such a way that it continued to fulfil its principal function of providing a separation between communities, while at the same time being defensible against further incursions.

The proposed scheme has successfully achieved a balance between the refurbishment of large areas of the green belt and remunerative development. New industrial and 'high-tech' uses have been accommodated on areas close to road accesses and adjacent to existing development. The new land uses have been designed to round off existing development thus creating a more defensible boundary to the green belt. The areas of new development have been designed to face onto the open space. The transition from development area to open space, and formal to informal, has been achieved through substantial boundary planting. There is direct access from the development sites to the Country Park. For example IBM, one of the office users, encourages employees to use the site as part of a 'health' walk.

The treatment of the open space areas can be divided into two types, north and south of the railway line. Within the northern part of the site the objective has been to break down the scale and inhospitable character of the site and improve the nature conservation value. Earth moving carried out in association with the earthworks programme has created a series of planted landforms which help to define new spaces or 'rooms'. These rooms are linked by a network of paths, bridleways and cycle/maintenance tracks. The size of these rooms varies from 0.5 to 3 hectares thus allowing a range of activities and events to take place. Two car parks are provided to serve the nature conservation area and a newly created fishing lake.

In the nature conservation areas the approach has involved:
- the maintenance of existing water associated habitats (for example open mud spit, reed beds, and willow carr) and the creation of new habitats (for example sandy banks for sand martins and a refuge island) for the existing lake;
- the formation of new lakes;
- the provision of a natural landscape backdrop to the areas of principal nature conservation interest;
- a mosaic of herb-rich meadow grassland, scrub and woodland blocks using native species once common to the area. Hounslow Heath provided some of the necessary context;
- the provision of an interpretation centre for use by schools, local groups and casual visitors.

The southern area is much less accessible to the public and it is intended that the land is made available to specialist recreation groups and high intensity users. The consultation exercise undertaken as part of the planning process identified a number of clubs interested in using the area (including junior motor cycle training and water sports) some of which were already using the site. Sound amelioration is provided by a 2.5 m high earth bund which acts as an acoustic barrier. The outer face of the bund is camouflaged by a band of wetland planting. Other uses provided for in the southern part of the site include water based activities, model boats, canoeing and sub-aqua diving. The local authority is currently consulting with local interest groups regarding the future management and use of this part of the scheme.

The overall approach to new planting has been to produce a landscape combining heath land, informal scrub, copse and shelter belt planting, as well as maintained field areas.

Access is controlled via two entrances which helps to maintain security. Some supervised activities are permitted in the evenings after normal closing.

Lake and office building construction

Earthworks Programme

A special feature of Bedfont Lakes has been the successful treatment of landfill material in situ. The methods adopted involved gathering all contaminated material in a central part of the site and sealing it within a clay cell. A system of wells and pumps transfers any contaminated substances from the cell directly into the foul sewer and a series of gas vents allows methane to escape. A second clay barrier around the perimeter of the site provides an additional layer of protection from contamination. Scientific analysis and monitoring indicates that this has been effective.

The earthworks operation involved recontouring the site and incorporating the clay cell as a mound within the central point of the site. A layer of topsoil across the site was sown with trees, shrubs and meadows in accordance with the natural heathland character prescribed for the site.

Management and Maintenance

Rutland Hall contributes to the cost of maintenance and management of the site through the transfer of a commuted sum to the council. Two of the existing occupiers and users also contribute to this fund. The annual maintenance cost is £150,000 which covers the provision of a ranger service, interpretation centre, landscape management and pollution control measures associated with the processing of in situ landfill gas. Four to six rangers are currently employed on the site, each of whom has a particular skill to supplement their core duties for example technical management, interpretation and ecology. The Country Park is supported by the Bedfont Lakes Ecological Advisory Committee which comprises local councillors, local authority officers, local wildlife groups, IBM as one of the site occupiers, and Rutland Hall. The intention is to make the park as sustainable as possible in the long term by, for example, using timber from the woodland for fencing, mulch and retaining edges for the water bodies.

FUNDING AND PARTNERS

Information boards and signage share common identity

- *Rutland Hall:* developer and part funder of maintenance and management of the site.
- *London Borough of Hounslow:* local planning authority during the process of implementation. The authority retains an involvement in the site in terms of consultation and management.
- *Community:* users, local interest groups, sports clubs.
- *IBM:* occupier of the site and revenue funder.

The approximate cost of the project, excluding development, was £15 million which was paid for by the private developer from the associated development.

LESSONS FOR GOOD PRACTICE

- The positive approach taken by London Borough of Hounslow to an area of despoiled green belt land and the use of planning agreements.
- The positive partnership arrangements between the local authority and developer helped to turn a liability into a positive asset.
- Landscape design including the regeneration of indigenous landscape, accommodation of nature conservation, passive and active recreation and a landscape which will be allowed to evolve over time.
- The comprehensive and integrated approach has allowed for new job creation, the provision of an attractive setting for industry and a new recreation and nature conservation resource for the community of West London.
- The successful processing and treatment of contaminated ground in situ, through on site processing of landfill gas and ensuring the sustainability of subsequent planting.

Contact: Colin Stuart, London Borough of Hounslow
The Civic Centre, Lampton Road, Hounslow, TW3 4DN

3.2 New Uses For Vacant Industrial Land (NUVIL), Knowsley

INTRODUCTION AND KEY ISSUES

In the mid 1980s Knowsley was suffering a prolonged period of industrial decline and the Borough Council acquired two large industrial estates from Liverpool City Council.

Before NUVIL project

De-industrialisation had produced a number of very large derelict sites which were proving expensive to maintain and which were unlikely to be attractive to inward or mobile investment in their current state. The NUVIL project was initiated to generate alternative uses for such land.

ACTION TAKEN

The project works by creating a partnership between the public sector (Knowsley Council) and the private sector (individual companies) with Groundwork St Helens, Knowsley and Sefton acting as the executive agency and intermediary.

The NUVIL project has simple objectives:

- to bring vacant industrial land back into productive use;
- to improve the condition of land and through this the image of the industrial sector;
- to create new employment opportunities in woodland creation and management and the timber industry;
- to increase the total amount of woodland in Knowsley;
- to research and measure the innovative approaches used by NUVIL.

The Groundwork Trust works with individual companies who own land to improve the quality of unused sections of that land with the overall intention of promoting the image of the company and improving the working environment for staff.

Improvements as part of NUVIL

The Trust offers Companies:

- generous local authority grant aid (50% via Groundwork);
- planting and design carried out by technical experts;
- full implementation of the project by the Trust;
- long term management of the planted areas;
- potential long term income.

This produces three types of treatment:

Long term woodland: this is on the fringes of sites, sites likely to remain undeveloped, or on sites for permanent planting.

Coppice woodland: on land which may be developed but which is unlikely to be developed in the short to medium term.

Biomass woodland: an experimental type of planting concentrating on areas likely to be developed in the short or medium term. Quick growing hybrids are encouraged which can be harvested every two/three years to provide wood chips for horticulture mulch or the raw material for power generation. Possibilities also exist for the production of willow for basket making.

In practice a 50/50 split on costs is agreed with 50% being grant aided and the remainder being paid by the individual company. The capital cost also includes money to fund a maintenance contract for the first three years after planting.

The average site cost for the development and planting is £2-2,500 an acre dependent on soil and other conditions. The returns from production are split in two ways. Short to medium term profit remains with NUVIL to be used for ongoing management, with long term returns going to the land owner.

If land is brought into use more rapidly than anticipated the land owner is not penalised if trees are removed. It recognises the need for flexibility and the fact that the NUVIL approach may have helped speed up the investment which requires the change of use.

Planting in Knowsley

FUNDING AND PARTNERS

Groundwork St. Helens, Knowsley and Sefton: the oldest and one of the largest of the 43 Groundwork Trusts in the UK with a wide range of environmental, social and economic activities.

The Business Community: the development of this project depends on the involvement of local businesses. Sites are only developed with the owner of the land and on the basis of at least part payment from the private company.

Knowsley Borough Council: an important source of finance and a major landowner in their own right on the industrial estate.

Mersey Forest Campaign: a major provider of support and joint publicity.

The cost of running this project is approximately £100,000 a year with income from grants, earned income and sale of biomass.

OUTCOMES

By December 1995 the project had:

Environmental improvements with innovative design

- treated 74 hectares of industrial land;
- planted more than 270,000 trees;
- planted 42 hectares of long term woodland;
- planted 13 hectares of coppice;
- planted 14 hectares of biomass;
- planted 5 hectares of wildflowers;
- held a major conference to promote the use of willow;
- held a joint conference to promote NUVIL (in partnership with Mersey Forest);
- cleared three sites for major industrial development;
- created 2.5 permanent jobs;
- played a major part in assisting Knowsley to achieve its Mersey Forest targets.

LESSONS FOR GOOD PRACTICE

The approach was considered highly innovative when first introduced and has subsequently been copied in many locations. Lessons learnt and transferred include:

- Greening can make a major difference to the value of, and public perception of, land in the area. The Council and Groundwork St Helen's, Knowsley and Sefton feel that the NUVIL work, along with other estate improvements made by the Council, played a major part in attracting at least three major companies to the area.

- Projects like these take time to mature. In the early stages of this project most of the land improved was Council owned. It was only as the improvements became obvious that the private sector was attracted.

- The approach to businesses must be business like. The NUVIL brochure is explicit in its appeal to the commercial interests of the companies involved, stressing the effects, among other things, on land values, maintenance costs, and employee morale of undertaking work of this sort.

- No attempt has been made to create a committee of business people. It is felt that business people do not want committees but want the right service provided at the right price. The 'committee' for the project is the Council and Groundwork working together.

- There is much wasted land around most factories which could be brought into productive use for the sake of the environment if not for the Company. Some sites may be held for potential expansion of the business, and could be suited to this sort of interim treatment.

- An environmental approach provides the opportunity for companies to involve the local community in their affairs. Many of the companies have involved local schools with the planting, design or maintenance of their sites.

Contact: Steve Freeman, Groundwork St Helen's, Knowsley and Sefton
19-27 Shaw Street, St Helen's, Merseyside, WA10 1DF

3.3 Shire Brook Valley, Sheffield

INTRODUCTION AND KEY ISSUES

In 1982, Sheffield City Council decided to set up a Countryside Management project for the Shire Brook Valley, aimed at turning an area of vacant derelict land blighted by disused sewage works and landfill, into a nature reserve. The site's many problems also included old colliery workings, fly tipping, motor-biking and poor access. Tree planting, footpath improvement and fencing had been undertaken at various times, mainly through MSC schemes. One of the principal focuses is the conversion of Coisley Hill Sewage Works, closed in 1990 and purchased from Yorkshire Water in December 1993.

ACTION TAKEN

The Council assembled the land, mostly through the use of Compulsory Purchase Orders and undertook extensive community consultation which led to the establishment of a new community group, the Shire Brook Conservation Group.

Coisley Hill sewage works

The aims as set out in the Management Plan were:

- to retain and enhance the landscape quality of the area;
- to protect and enhance areas of natural history and industrial archaeology;
- to create areas of active open space;
- to contain industrial development to those areas in existing use;
- to provide on and off site interpretation to enhance the enjoyment of visitors;
- to provide facilities for continuing educational use of the valley's resources;
- to provide a protected network of footpaths, cycleways and bridleways throughout the valley;
- to eliminate the pollution in the Shire Brook;
- to ensure early cessation of tipping activities in the valley linked to rapid landscape reclamation;
- to prevent abuse by motor cycles, fly tipping and vandalism.

Specific design objectives included: making the area safe; maximising opportunities for recycling, for example grinding up the old concrete tanks for use on the footpaths and adapting the tank gantries to make bridges for the brook.

Strategic Context

Strategically, the Shire Brook Valley Countryside Management Plan (CAMP) fits into the wider context of the Green Belt Plan for Sheffield, which was adopted in 1983; the Access to Sheffield's Countryside policy statement (approved 1987); the Strategy for Countryside Management in Sheffield (1987); and the Nature Conservation Strategy adopted in 1991. Proposals from the management plan were also included in the City's Unitary Development Plan. The consultation process was intended to increase awareness about the resource, identify the main conflicts and problems, and to find solutions.

The CAMP went through some formal public consultation in March 1984 and May 1989, with an exhibition and series of public meetings, but the plan was never formally approved. A revised plan has been drawn up to continue improvements.

Community Involvement

Activities such as clean up schemes, and tree planting involving local residents and school children, guided walks (with themes such as industrial archaeology) and activity days were used to generate interest in the first instance.

Relationships with schools were developed gradually. Contacts with head teachers focused initially on practical issues: how to *do* some simple things in school grounds, such as tree nurseries. This gradually changed perceptions, and helped to build relationships, but four years were needed to develop local specialist interest to the point where it became 'self-starting'.

The interest of local councillors and the press was also actively cultivated. Community involvement began with residents' associations on the estates that skirt the valley and encouraging fundraising activities. Key sites, such as Carr Forge Dam (a striking water feature which attracts local interest), Nether Wheel (a site of major industrial archaeological interest) and the Old Railway Line were targeted first so as to create an early impact.

The Shire Brook Conservation Group (SCG) was set up with support from the Countryside Management Service. Volunteers from the Group carry out a variety of conservation tasks, working with the Countryside Unit. Several members have been trained as voluntary rangers.

Birley Spa, the only Victorian Bath House now left in South Yorkshire, is owned by the Council and forms part of the plan (the Birley Spa Vale). The SCG and local schools have helped the Countryside Management Service with native tree and shrub planting, access improvements and clean ups. The site has scope to become an interpretation centre, an educational resource, ranger service base and major visitor attraction. The SCG use the Spa for their meetings, and it has become available for wider community use.

Project Officer's Role

The project officer's role is a crucial part of the process. She acts as initiator and enabler for many tasks, working with the people who live in and manage the land and those who visit the countryside.

As part of her job the project officer:

- provides a focal point for local initiatives and acts as a bridge between local people and the various agencies and departments of local and central government;

Shire Brook's new flower meadows

- establishes close links with land managers and local people in quite a large area, and from these develops a good understanding of its problems (this is important as the City Council does not own all of the land involved);

- takes action to resolve problems and conflicts of land management (appropriate contacts can be alerted quickly, for instance, when there is slight evidence of pollution, so that bigger problems can be averted);

- devises and develops a longer term programme of work to resolve more complex issues (for instance tactics to reduce air rifle use and motor bike access, through detailed discussion with the police and strategic early use of fencing at key access points);

- develops conservation and recreation opportunities as quickly and effectively as possible, paying particular attention to the needs of disadvantaged groups;

- is a source of advice on grants and official requirements (for example what procedures need to be followed with listed buildings such as the Spa);

- stimulates and co-ordinates the interest and involvement of voluntary groups, schools and communities in the improvement of an area;

- together with the implementation officer, provides direction and training opportunities for volunteers and temporarily employed labour. Having worked as a local volunteer herself, the project officer has a feel for what it is reasonable to expect of volunteers and what support they need; when training takes place, for example through BTCV, it often involves the project team, so their capabilities are extended. Training has included ranger training, fence and gate construction, tree and hedge planting, hedge laying, drystone walling, risk assessment, but form-filling, for example for grant applications, has not yet been tackled;

- is a source of advice and intelligence to local and central government officials on the problems of the area;

- fosters greater care and understanding of the countryside, particularly among young people.

FUNDING

The initial budget was approximately £15,000 plus staff time and overheads, but the local authority has developed a flexible and creative approach to generating support.

Shire Brook Valley after the sewage work conversion

Initially 50% grant aid and advice came from the Countryside Commission and Forestry Authority (Woodland Grants Scheme), and then further funding for specific projects in 1986-7; English Partnerships and Derelict Land Grant funding (£331,000 for sewage plant); Transpennine, Millennium funding and European Regional Development Fund. Other smaller contributors, include British Gas, McDonalds and Yorkshire Electricity;

There is currently a five year funded maintenance contract for the former sewage works site, but what will happen beyond that is not clear.

PARTNERS

The Shire Brook Conservation Group: the capabilities of the group have been developed to a point where it can take responsibility for carrying out many of the maintenance and monitoring tasks: in many cases the Council needs only now to provide the materials while the group provides the manpower. Volunteer activities include meadow management, footpath maintenance, bracken control, wetland management, hedge and tree planting;

Sheffield City Council: participation from various departments in the steering group and on a day to day basis is the key to heading off problems, exploring new ideas and tackling big issues that demand a multi-department/agency approach, such as how to deal with the old sewage plant;

British Trust for Conservation Volunteers: involvement in training activities in particular;

Sheffield University; Rotherham and Maltby Conservation;

Yorkshire Electricity: putting special markers on power lines that were a danger to landing swans;

British Gas and McDonalds in sponsoring various activities;

Government Office for Yorkshire and Humberside have advised over specific European Regional Development Fund and English Partnerships matters.

The TEC: individuals may receive grants from the TEC for Environmental Training Scheme (SET), and one training event of this sort has been run each year. The initiative also had a Youth Training programme (15 full time trainees), but since the demise of Community Programme, opportunities for the TEC to fund this type of training activity have become scarce.

OUTCOMES

The valley is to be formally designated as a Local Nature Reserve, and the Conservation Group has developed considerably; they together with the wider community participate actively in maintenance and management. Visitors to the Nature Reserve include not just local residents, but also people from all over Sheffield and beyond.

Shire Brook Conservation Group and volunteers at work by one of the interpretation boards

The Steering Group, known as the South East Countryside Management Advisory Group continues to meet three or four times a year to guide the project team. An implementation officer works with the volunteers and has a skills development role. Technical problems remain, for example water quality, which would require massive investment by Yorkshire Water. Fly tipping, mine water leach and the active landfill site continue to pose problems for the managers.

The Conservation Group has started monitoring the numbers of species of plant in the newly sown meadows. The trees are clearly growing well - particularly around the sewage plant - although some are needing to be replaced after vandalism.

Quantifiable achievements of the South East Sheffield Countryside Management Area, between April 1995 and March 1996 include the following:

- 19 schools involved in environmental education;
- 350 local children involved in practical conservation work;
- 1,091 volunteer days' work;
- 101 tons of rubbish removed;
- 1,050 metres of mixed native hedge planted;
- 1,500 native trees planted;
- 2,000 native bulbs planted;
- 18 hectares of wildflower meadow managed;
- 7 bird feeding stations created;
- record number of birds over winter at Carr Forge Dam;
- wetland management at 12 ponds;
- 90 metres of path improvements;
- one new Countryside Stewardship scheme approved;
- Gleadless Valley Management Plan (Phase One) approved by Committee;
- Official Opening of Shire Brook Valley Nature Reserve;
- Pair of kingfishers seen in the valley;
- 1.5 hectares of lowland heath managed;
- 211 metres of low fencing;
- 62 metres of dry-stone walling;
- 251 metres of hedge laying;
- two new boardwalks and one new car park built at Beighton Marsh;
- two visitor surveys at Richmond Park;
- 400 dumped tyres removed from Shire Brook Valley;
- with Countryside Management Service support, the Fishponds Action Group was formed;
- 33 press articles, with other tv, local and national radio coverage;
- 40 events and activities, organised, attended by 2,500 people.

The project officer on one of the new bridges made from parts of the former sewage works

LESSONS FOR GOOD PRACTICE

- The mix of expertise has been important: the knowledge of the land, farming techniques and the seasons by one key member of the group has been used well, as have company contacts.
- Early 'focal points' were significant in stimulating local interest, particularly the water features.
- The whole process was deliberately and explicitly founded on consultation, to develop a sense of local ownership and encourage use.
- Continuity of staffing has been helpful in that the first project officer became the project team leader.
- Consideration needs to be given to medium term revenue funding issues.
- Informal support (sometimes at the local pub) has been important, and knowledge/experience of volunteering locally has been significant in being able to judge what it was appropriate for volunteers to tackle, and the support likely to be required.
- The team, SCG and the steering group will be able to use the experiences in Shire Brook Valley to develop other city greening projects. The fact that it is part of a citywide strategy will assist this.
- Political support has added important weight to the process, through councillors and MPs.

- Insurance is an important consideration in relation to the volunteers. The SCG is acting on behalf of the Council here, and would thus be covered by the Council's arrangements, but the fullest possible cover and health and safety training are crucial.
- It is important to cultivate the press and encourage co-operation.
- Similar projects need to cultivate the police and fire services early on. Their co-operation and preventive work, with schools and, for the former, plain clothes work, is essential, as much of the success could easily be undone by a fire or by the return of air rifles and motor bikes to the valley.
- Continuity is essential in work with schools, so that generations do not miss out on exposure to the issues which will help them to develop a sense of stewardship.

Contact: Sally Pereira, Countryside Management Unit
         Sheffield City Council, Town Hall, Sheffield, S1 2HH

3.4 Sheepwash Urban Park, Sandwell

INTRODUCTION AND KEY ISSUES

Sheepwash Urban Park, forerunner to the Urban Forest Strategy, provides an example of an ambitious regeneration project involving the reclamation of a contaminated landfill site for open space following naturalistic rather than formal processes.

As derelict land, its ability to attract bad neighbour uses is a common problem. The case study provides an interesting example in terms of the approach to reclamation, involving relatively low cost techniques and leading to the rapid transformation of the image of an area.

ACTION TAKEN

Initiation

The Sheepwash site, situated at the heart of the West Midlands Urban Area, adjacent to the Birmingham Canal and the Wolverhampton-Birmingham railway line, has a long industrial history which includes coal-mining, sand and gravel extraction and more recently, the disposal of industrial and domestic waste.

The ending of landfill activity left Sandwell Metropolitan Borough Council with a large tract of derelict land containing contaminated waste and waste capable of producing landfill gas, which had a major blighting affect on the image of the area. The Council realised that without intervention, the site could affect the surrounding residential areas with atmospheric pollution and the leaching of contaminants.

Early site investigations concluded that the site was unsuitable for immediate industrial or residential development and that the adjacent River Tame would need large scale remediation works to prevent future flooding. These two factors and the fact that the area lacked open space suggested that the site should be reclaimed for open space to provide a strategic amenity resource for local people.

Strategy Development

Following an early round of public consultation, Sandwell MBC decided to begin the reclamation of the site. The approach was to accelerate the process of natural regeneration. The four stages of reclamation illustrate the incremental way in which reclamation took place over time:

- the treatment of all mineshafts, the provision of a methane cut-off trench, the import of topsoil and the final restoration of one part of the site;
- river improvement and flood control works. At the same time, a large part of the site was planted, a new access road was provided together with footpaths, fencing and drainage works;
- a final phase of planting on the main site area, including earthworks, tree planting and seeding;
- works to the pool areas and the areas affected by the river.

Implementation

A cross-disciplinary working party was set-up for the implementation and subsequent management of the project, comprising engineers, planners, landscape architects and ecologists from various departments within the council. Although no department had specific overall responsibility for the project, the planning department, and in particular one officer, became responsible for the overall co-ordination and implementation of the various projects over its ten year life. It was felt that while this multi-disciplinary working has allowed issues to be addressed in an appropriate manner using the skills required, such an arrangement tended to focus the team's attention on individual projects, at the risk of losing sight of the overall scheme. Political support through the process has also been lacking, which has affected the funding of the project, in that the officers have had to rely almost entirely on external funding sources.

Sheepwash Urban Park improvements

Consultation has been a key element of the project's planning, design and implementation. Groups such as the West Midlands-based Urban Wildlife Group, the then Nature Conservancy Council (English Nature), the Royal Society for the Protection of Birds, the Countryside Commission and Sandwell Valley Field Naturalists Club all provided advice in relation to planting techniques, layout, and the retention of the main pools together with the wetland areas. The main emphasis of all these organisations was, however, that the site should not become a 'green desert', punctuated with standard and ornamental trees.

Pool areas after improvements

Community Involvement

The design and layout of the Park has involved extensive consultation with nature conservation groups. There has, however, been limited day-to-day public involvement. Local community needs and desires have not been taken on board in the design process. However, the extent of change that was being proposed and the lack of alternatives for the site in the short-term suggested that community consultation on the future use of the site would be of limited value. Residents have, however, been kept informed throughout the process via newsletters and some of the planting has been undertaken by the National Urban Forestry Unit, with help from school children. The BTCV has undertaken several projects on the site including planting, island creation and fence building.

FUNDING AND PARTNERS

Reclamation of the site was given approval by the DoE in July 1978. Work did not, however, begin until 1982. A working partnership between West Midlands County Council as part landowner, Sandwell MBC as part owner and part implementing agency and South Tame Water Authority as implementation agent of the River Tame flood prevention scheme, brought about a cost saving to the DoE of an estimated £118,000 through co-ordinated work practices. The primary source of funding was Derelict Land Grant (funded at 100% instead of the previous 50% maximum) and the Black Country Development Corporation. The scheme was phased over a ten year period.

The phased approach to funding of the scheme has allowed for a number of benefits and disbenefits to emerge. On the one hand, the need to justify the use of DLG at each stage has allowed plans and ideas to develop properly. However, each phase has tended to become a project in itself, in terms of its design, funding and implementation, and the resulting incremental approach diverts attention from the long-term aims of the project as a whole.

LESSONS FOR GOOD PRACTICE

- The availability of capital grants to support the physical reclamation and decontamination of sites is important.
- The emphasis on encouraging natural regeneration provides a longer term, more self sustaining approach to reclamation.
- Community participation ensures local relevance and hence longevity of the project.
- Reclamation methods which minimise capital costs as well as maintenance costs can be adopted.

Contact: Chris Blakey, Sandwell Metropolitan Borough Council
        PO Box 46, "Wigmore", Penyhill Lane, West Bromwich, B71 3RZ

3.5 Blackbrook Valley
incorporating Saltwells Local Nature Reserve, Dudley

INTRODUCTION AND KEY ISSUES

The Blackbrook Valley, situated in Dudley, provides an example of an environmentally based regeneration project which sought to develop a comprehensive landscape strategy for a vast area of derelict and abused land, incorporating an ancient woodland and an Enterprise Zone.

ACTION TAKEN

Strategy Development

The area was incorporated within the Dudley (Brierley Hill) Enterprise Zone in 1981, at the same time the site was selected as a demonstration project under the European Campaign for Urban Renaissance (1980). Saltwells Wood was designated as a Local Nature Reserve (LNR) in 1981, giving it special protection.

Both the Enterprise Zone and the Urban Renaissance concept were experimental and potentially conflicting. It was argued at the time, however, that the adoption of the ecological aims of the Urban Renaissance Project within the Enterprise Zone could provide an example of the benefits of starting with landscape design and integrating industry and people *within* it rather than the more usual approach of incorporating 'greening' as an artificial afterthought.

The broad aim of the project was to attempt an experimental approach where the best techniques of environmental improvement could be used within a framework of full community involvement (Dudley MBC 1982). The more detailed aims of the project were:

- to conserve and enhance the existing landscape and drainage of the valley;
- to minimise the impact of development/redevelopment on the valley's ecology by identifying and protecting areas of special natural importance and by taking ecological principles into account in design and management;
- to ensure that management proposals for the valley were defined in the context of the design of landscape treatments;
- to encourage the use of the area as an educational resource;
- to use the landscape improvements survey and environmental monitoring work in the valley to increase community involvement in decision making, self help and long term management.

A steering committee, known as the Blackbrook Valley Project Team, was established to supervise the project's evolution. It consisted of representatives of various participating organisations and local interest groups, including the NCC (now English Nature), the County Council, the DoE, the Countryside Commission and the National Coal Board (now British Coal).

Although a formal and detailed management plan was not drawn up until 1986, the Blackbrook Valley Project Team (BVPT) did draw up a masterplan which was approved in June 1981. The plan was valley-wide and brought together a number of detailed policies which built on the original objectives including that:

- the framework for the development should be provided through the creation or enhancement of a network of ecological corridors;
- natural drainage and ground-water should be maintained where possible;
- only native species should be planted;
- voluntary groups and the local community groups should be encouraged for all projects;
- the scope for employment and training should be considered for all projects;
- education should play a major role in the project;
- management proposals should be clearly defined before assessing development and long-term management implications;
- access for the local community should be enhanced and safety improved.

For the proposed private sector development within the Enterprise Zone the masterplan urged developers to: minimise landscape reshaping; retain hedgerows as boundaries between or within sites; minimise 'skyline development'; use embankments between building platforms to create ecological corridors; use temporary or vacant sites for nature conservation; and adopt a heavy planting policy for car parks and other areas of unsightly development. Housing developers were encouraged to: use landscape strategy plans based on existing vegetation, as a basis for development; carry out advance planting of trees and shrubs, forming belts where possible; exploit views out of the site; allocate space for tree-planting; ensure that changes in ground-water would not affect existing vegetation; develop areas for informal play with landscape areas; and involve residents in the project at the earliest possible stage.

Each of the above objectives and requirements provide a framework for best practice for those producing a landscape strategy. However, in the implementation process of this particular project, the annual report noted in 1983 that, whilst the LNR and Claypit had been progressed quickly and in accordance with the masterplan by wardens employed on the site, the private sector had failed totally to co-operate with the project aims which applied to them, even though Dudley MBC had set up a Landscape Advisory Service to offer free advice to developers in the area.

Community Involvement

The process of resident involvement has been successful and can largely be attributed to the prolonged and determined efforts of wardens.

The residential community were not consulted at the outset of the project, rather the involvement has been generated through implementation, primarily because the site's physical characteristics prevented any other form of development which seemed to render a detailed assessment of local needs irrelevant. In addition, it was felt that the novelty of such a scheme in an area of industrial decline might well have provoked a less than enthusiastic response from local people had they been formally consulted.

The appointment of an appropriate Senior Landscape Warden was seen as being critical to the success of the project. The BVPT decided that rather than appoint a warden with an appropriate academic qualification, they would appoint a warden whose background included agricultural training and police work. The warden's long-standing interest in natural history, together with his ability to stamp his authority on the site, are recognised as fundamentally important by all those involved in the project.

Management

The management plan provides a framework to guide the future development of the LNR. The availability of wardens on the site allows this plan to be implemented in a flexible and responsive manner, depending upon the circumstances that arise on the site, man-made or natural.

FUNDING AND PARTNERS

Although continued funding for this project has been precarious and difficult to achieve, the project has benefited from the fact that a number of short-term funding regimes favoured this particular project type (including Derelict Land Grant and Urban Aid). However, as with a number of projects, project officers were at times faced with the problem of fitting long-term aims to short-term grant budgets. As the 1982 Annual Report noted, "this sometimes encouraged too much work, too quickly."

Management of the LNR largely depended in the early years on staff employed through a Council sponsored MSC Community Programme scheme. Demise of this programme resulted in their replacement by three permanent council posts, including the appointment of a Senior Warden. The site today is managed by five wardens whose roles include maintenance, patrol, management, education and community liaison. The cost (inclusive of salaries and running costs of the Education Centre) is approximately £100,000 per annum allocated through Dudley MBC's revenue budgets.

OUTCOMES

- Success can be measured in the form of residents acting as unofficial wardens, the amount of time committed by residents to projects, together with the reduction in vandalism and fly tipping. The continuity of warden involvement has also contributed significantly to the project's success in terms of sustaining local confidence.

- The creation of Saltwells Wood has, in essence, been about the safeguarding and enhancement of existing ecological habitats, and their management in a soundly based manner. Such an approach has led to the creation of robust environments which are easier to manage and maintain in the long term.

LESSONS FOR GOOD PRACTICE

- The contribution of the various participants has been diverse and interlocking. It is an example of collaborative and multi-disciplinary working between individuals with a variety of different skills and roles but who were committed to the project's success.

- The project has enjoyed a high degree of political support throughout its life, which has contributed significantly to its realisation.

- The lack of planning controls in the Enterprise Zone, together with a lack of incentive among developers and landowners to become involved in environmental projects prevented development from being integrated in landscape terms with the open space in the valley.

- Community involvement has been built up through the sustained efforts of the warden. Projects have been carefully designed and implemented to attract the interest and involvement of local people. Large scale projects which would have an immediate effect on the environment were implemented first in order to attract attention and initiate contact. Close contact was made with school children who are likely to watch over and protect the environment and who are able to influence parents who may have been suspicious of the project.

- The appointment of a warden whose talents allowed him to involve local people while maintaining firm authority, rather than a biologist or ecologist, has proved to be very effective in improving the community's perception of the project.

- The establishment of the BVPT has ensured cross departmental communication between the different organisations involved in the project. The project benefited from the involvement of many different organisations offering a diverse range of skills and ideas.

- The project benefited from the flexible attitude towards the use of Derelict Land Grant and the reclamation of land for open space use as opposed to hard end uses. However, the project also suffered from the uncertainty created by the short termism of many of the grant regimes which forced the implementation of works at inappropriate stages in the project's development while at the same time threatening the project's longevity.

- The project benefited from an in-depth knowledge of the local ecology which provided the basis for well-informed management decisions.

Contacts: Ian Jeavons/Sue Timms, Dudley Metropolitan Borough Council
       Planning and Leisure Department, St James Road, Dudley, West Midlands, DY1 1HZ

3.6 Bold Moss, St Helen's

INTRODUCTION AND KEY ISSUES

In 1987, Bold Moss Colliery in St Helen's was closed and the surface buildings converted to managed workspace by a consortium of the local council, local enterprise agency and British Coal Enterprise. Spoil from the colliery had been tipped on Bold Moss, one of the last remnants of wetlands which at one time covered most of the Lancashire plain. Although much of the Moss had been destroyed, significant wetland areas remained on the margins of the tip. However, they were being degraded as a result of toxic waste seeping from the spoil tip. The tip was inaccessible and had a significant blighting affect on the surrounding community.

Bold Moss: a bridge to its mining past

A condition attached to the original planning consent required British Coal to treat the tip on cessation of waste dumping. Preliminary assessments suggested that the tip be reclaimed for recreational purposes. In pursuit of this suggestion the local authority and British Coal employed the local Groundwork Trust to establish a reclamation programme for the area.

ACTION TAKEN

Active involvement of the local community was seen as the key to the project's long term success. The community, however, had very little knowledge of the area, or sense of ownership as the tip had been inaccessible and in a degraded state for a significant period of time.

The process was started in 1989 when approximately 50 hectares of land, which incorporated the tip, was sold by British Coal to a newly established trust for £1. The sale agreement also included the payment of a £500,000 dowry to the trust to pay for any work to be undertaken.

Groundwork had established two simple objectives in its early years:

- to use the site as a laboratory for the renovation of coal spoil tips and wetlands and convert them into productive, or at least environmentally friendly, areas;
- to improve the quality of the land.

It soon became clear, however, that there was potential for a wider programme of activity. To work effectively as an environmental project Groundwork decided to:

- involve the local community and expand their knowledge and capacity so that they could become effective partners;
- improve the total environment over a stretch of 150 hectares, thus generating land for housing and commercial use;
- enhance the environment of an important town gateway.

It was also realised that there could be a series of benefits from the proper handling of this project in terms of:

- an increase in the confidence of the people in the area;
- an improvement in external perceptions of the area;
- a supply of good quality and popular training and volunteering places.

Bold Moss Welcome Stone

To enable these wider objectives to be realised Groundwork established a Bold Moss Forum composed of local residents, Councillors and Groundwork members to oversee the project.

Extensive discussions then took place with the local community who adopted naturalistic planting techniques, promoting diverse landscapes and habitats as opposed to monotone grassed areas. The approach, which is slow and measured, was to work with the restorative forces of nature and take advantage of the features and species that were already in place.

Opportunities were created for local people to be involved actively and schools worked on the Moss as part of their community and national curriculum activities. Wherever possible, specific groups were encouraged to make their uses for the area known and to take some, or all, of the responsibility for certain parts of the project. Thus anglers became involved on one site and bikers on another.

FUNDING AND PARTNERS

- *Groundwork St. Helen's/Knowsley and Sefton:* the oldest and one of the largest of over 40 Groundwork Trusts in the UK, with a range of environmental, social and economic activities;

- *The community:* an important source of knowledge, ideas, inspiration and volunteers. They are, above all, the intended end users of the project;

Bold Moss

- *The Department of the Environment:* DoE is a core funder of the Groundwork Trust movement;

- *St. Helen's Metropolitan Borough Council:* an important source of finance and assistance with integration with the local community;

- *National Power:* source of funds for renovation of the former power station site;

- *British Coal:* source of funds for the renovation of the spoil heap.

To date the trust has spent approximately £800,000 which has come from a wide variety of sources. This includes money from the Countryside Commission, Europe, St. Helen's Metropolitan Borough Council, British Coal and the Department of the Environment (through the Derelict Land Grant and the Single Regeneration Budget Challenge Fund).

Bold Moss wetlands

It should be noted that £400,000 of the original Coal Board dowry still remains and has been invested to provide finance for ongoing care and maintenance.

Expansion will also have the potential to generate funds from the lottery and National Power for the redevelopment of the former power station site. The expanded area will require a budget of £3,000,000.

OUTCOMES

Not all of the project's outputs for this project fall within the tight definitions of the Challenge Fund and similar regimes. The project has, however:

- partially reclaimed 50 hectares of ground;
- developed new land reclamation techniques for dealing with redundant tips;
- encouraged more than 500 volunteers to take part in environmental activities;
- trained 30 people to NVQ2 level;
- promoted diversity of flora and fauna;
- helped stimulate the development of the local community;
- encouraged 'greening' of the surrounding residential environment;
- influenced the policies and proposals contained within the St. Helen's Unitary Development Plan.

LESSONS FOR GOOD PRACTICE

- The community constitutes a major player in environmental activity and not just a user of the finished product. They can contribute initiative, non-specific knowledge, volunteers, continuity and a market research role for the end use.

- Innovative, non-standard techniques for landscape establishment are possible which support variety in terms of planting, habitat and use.

- Major projects like this often have a very long lead time. In this case six years elapsed from the approval of a local plan to the first movement of earth. Long term commitment of funding, skills and time are pre-requisites for projects of this scale and complexity.

- Reclamation and subsequent greening can make a major difference to the value of, and public perception of, land in the area.

- While it is not usually possible to quantify the economic development benefits of this work there is a clear feeling among the partners that improving gateways and removing dereliction improves inward investment and improves local employee satisfaction.

Bold Moss improvements

Contact: Groundwork St Helen's
Knowsley and Sefton, 19-27 Shaw Street, St Helen's, Merseyside WA10 1DF.

4.1 Premier Business Park, Walsall

INTRODUCTION AND KEY ISSUES

Premier Business Park is a 1970s industrial estate located a mile off the M6 in Walsall in the West Midlands. The estate comprises some forty small and medium enterprises (SMEs) in a variety of mainly tennanted and freehold premises.

Premier Business Park before the work began

By the mid 1980s, what had originally been intended as a high quality location had deteriorated and crime and vandalism had increased dramatically. The businesses were faced with stark choices, either to sell up and leave, or stay and take action to turn the estate around and protect their investment.

They chose the latter and ten years later the enhancement of the physical environment and the improvement in company performance has made Premier Business Park a successful example of what can be achieved on a small to medium scale industrial estate faced with typical problems of urban decline.

ACTION TAKEN

Initiation

In 1985, the businesses decided to take collective action against the problems of crime, vandalism and environmental degradation being experienced on the estate. They formed an Estates Committee with assistance from the Chamber of Commerce and began the process of extensive lobbying of officials. Despite their efforts, the estate remained in a run down state.

In 1990, Groundwork Black Country were invited by the Chamber of Commerce to assist in developing a comprehensive strategy for upgrading the estate's environment.

The approach adopted by Groundwork to the environmental regeneration of Premier Business Park was an holistic one, combining the physical enhancement of the environment with assistance to companies to improve their environmental performance, in ways that would allow them to make financial savings.

The physical enhancement of the environment

Groundwork were given a specific brief to undertake consultations and produce a masterplan to improve the environment around the park.

The starting point for this master planning exercise was to consult with each business individually. This exercise identified a number of collective problems including crime, vandalism, litter, security and the poor image of the estate.

In parallel, Groundwork undertook their own analysis of the estate and consulted with the police in order to identify the problems and opportunities that existed.

The results of the consultation exercise and the analysis were reviewed and formed the basis for the production of a masterplan and costings aimed at the comprehensive upgrading of the estate. Issues addressed by the plan included:

Before the enhancements

- security;
- floodlighting of service yards;
- poor quality street lighting;
- the treatment of boundaries and edges, building entrances, 'gateways' into the sites;
- the condition of the roads, footways and traffic calming;
- overnight lorry parking;
- car parking;
- litter and vandalism.

The primary aim of the scheme design was to create a cohesive image for the park and to improve its operation in terms of rationalising land uses, car parking, pedestrian and vehicular movement / conflict, servicing and access and security.

Measures in the scheme included:

- the definition of service yards and the provision of security fencing and flood lighting;
- simple planting combining low to medium scale groundcover shrubs and tree planting, replacing concrete forecourts and unkempt grass areas which formed the perimeter of each block;
- resurfacing of roads and the provision of traffic calming measures;
- planting to reinforce entry points into the site;
- defining spaces and ownership through the use of paving materials and planting;
- new street lighting and resurfacing of pedestrian routes;
- providing bollards to prevent overnight lorry parking on pavements.

The scheme was used as the basis upon which to bid for Urban Programme funding via Walsall Metropolitan Borough Council.

After: new perimeter planting, and planting at key entrance points

Environmental Audit

Following the physical enhancement work, the businesses were offered the opportunity to be the subject of an environmental review. This is a service offered by Groundwork, funded by City Challenge (50%) and with additional support from Environmental Regional Development Fund (ERDF).

These reviews provided advice on how the internal environment of the businesses could be managed to its financial advantage. For example, Power Utilities, which makes industrial filter products for major UK manufacturers and operates from a site within the Park, expected to save around £3,000 on lighting, site maintenance, packaging materials and cleaning in the year following their review. Staff also enjoy much better working conditions because of improvements in air quality and noise reduction. The company is now looking at the possibility of working up to BS 7750.

FUNDING AND PARTNERS

- *Premier Business Park Ltd;* established in 1985, a company limited by guarantee comprising representatives from the businesses. The success of the company lies in the enthusiasm and pro-active nature of its members.

In addition to their contribution to capital works, many members pay up to £450 a year into a 'green fund' which contributes towards upgrading the Park. It was suggested that this sign of commitment helped to sway grant giving bodies, such as English Partnerships and the ERDF, in their favour.

The partnership is continuously evolving and meets regularly with the police, local council and other agencies. One businessman mentioned that the organisation and process had engendered a real sense of community on the estate which has led to a potential for a mini supply chain being established for exchange of products and ideas. A primary objective of the organisation in the future is to expand these linkages through group insurance, internal joint training schemes and the provision of a collective waste management system on site.

- *Groundwork Black Country;* acted as the catalyst and facilitator in the process of involving the business community and responding to their needs; producing a strategic masterplan for the park's future development; identifying funding sources; submitting bids in partnership with other organisations; sending out tenders; and undertaking contractor administration.

As the process has evolved, Groundwork's role has reduced as the partnership between landowners strengthens and they become more confident and knowledgeable of dealing with their problems. Groundwork today acts as technical advisor.

- *East Mercia Chamber of Commerce;* provided the businesses with advice and administrative support in the initial stages of the organisation, and in 1995 in conjunction with Walsall City Challenge, funded the appointment of a Business Coordinator, whose brief is to manage the estate along with two other estates.

- *Walsall Metropolitan Borough Council;* have provided technical support and advice on a number of issues including lighting and maintenance. A mainstream local authority programme for roads maintenance and street lighting was coordinated with the programme of improvements as a result of the local authority's, close involvement and support.

- *City Challenge;* has provided finance for capital works and the sponsoring of Environmental Audits.

Perimeter tree and shrub planting of industrial areas within the Black Country

Total investment to date amounts to £471,952 which has come from the Urban Programme, City Challenge, the European Regional Development Fund, Walsall Metropolitan Borough Council, English Partnerships and the businesses on the estate. Maintenance costs of £5,700pa are paid for by contributions from the businesses on the estate.

OUTCOMES

- Substantial reduction in the incidents of crime and vandalism;
- Public perception that the risk of crime had substantially decreased;
- Public / private sector leverage (£470,000 public funding leading to £5.25 million from the private sector);
- Increased value of properties;
- Significant reduction in levels of vacancy.

LESSONS FOR GOOD PRACTICE

- A change and upgrading of physical image acted as the short term catalyst to encourage greater involvement.

- The partnership arrangements established by the project provided the necessary combination of skills and ensured that actions were targeted appropriately and at the right time. The commitment of the individual owners and their collective action provided the catalyst to encourage further investment.

- The creation of a strategic master plan provided the mechanism with which to attract external funds and tackle a whole host of problems and issues in a comprehensive and coordinated manner.

- An holistic approach to environmental regeneration encouraged internal cost savings and sustainable approaches to business management.

- The involvement of an external facilitator (Groundwork Black Country in this case) provided the local business community with the technical skills they lacked.

- A committed individual given the support of strong partners provided the key to the success of a difficult initiative.

- The process takes longer than conventional approaches, but is likely to be more sustainable now that the framework for consultation and mechanisms for long term management have been established.

Contact: Melanie Walters, Groundwork Black Country
       West Midlands House, Gipsy Lane, Willenhall, West Midlands, WV13 2HA

4.2 Amoco's CATS Gas Terminal Project, Teesmouth

INTRODUCTION AND KEY ISSUES

This project is distinctive for its approach to 'total quality' and collaboration. The first UK gas pipeline direct to an industrial area took on the challenge of being in, and next to, environmentally and scientifically protected areas of Teesmouth. CATS is a joint venture, involving a group of companies and being operated on their behalf by Amoco.

In taking the project forward, the CATS project team is :

Dune restoration on Coatham Sands

'...committed to expanding the Central Area Transmission System to provide facilities setting the global standard for safety, operating flexibility, reliability and cost, while creating positive environmental impact....through extraordinary performance, communication and successful partnerships, utilising the innovation and full potential of all project participants.'

Teesmouth was declared a National Nature Reserve (NNR) by English Nature in March 1995, comprising 340 hectares of intertidal flats, dunes, saltmarsh and grazing marsh, supporting high densities of wildfowl and wading birds. Located within a Site of Special Scientific Interest (SSSI), the CATS project team was keen to work positively within the constraints of its special designation, helping English Nature to enhance opportunities for the area, and setting its vision as a benchmark for the onshore construction industry. Thus, environment, health and safety have been key leadership themes for Amoco, and environmental and community consultation issues have formed an integral part of the investment and strategy from the outset.

ACTION TAKEN

The three phase plant development has been thought through in partnership with English Nature and INCA (Industry and Nature Conservation Association) from the very early stages to maximise the opportunities for *designing* in good environmental practice. Examples of this include:

- extensive site survey work early on, to identify exactly what flora and fauna should be preserved;

- restricting the times when piling (which causes noise and vibration) takes place so as not to disturb nesting birds;

- designing a rain water soakaway as a mini wetland (using reed beds as a natural purifier) complementing a neighbouring wetland reserve area;

- choosing a gravel size which would encourage ringed plovers to nest on an otherwise barren area, which could not be greened over;

- selective grass mowing, within the constraints of fire regulations, to protect some wild species;

- developing staff video training materials on themes such as 'environmental compliance' and 'environmental awareness for engineers'.

Consultation

The team went through an exhaustive process of consultation, including presentations to the local authorities, the Health and Safety Executive, the National River Authority, Her Majesty's Inspectorate of Pollution and the local planning authorities setting out clearly what was being planned or considered, and seeking feedback, advice and ideas on the proposals. This took place at the pre-planning stage, so that blockages and anxieties

Landfall point for the CATS pipeline, near Redcar

were kept to a minimum. Environmental bodies were consulted via English Nature, whose officer had built up a good understanding of the project. The pipeline route had been walked with INCA and English Nature, to see what might be disturbed. Other consultees included the Police, Cleveland Wildlife Trust, neighbouring firms, the Civil Aviation Authority (because of the height of the structure), the Crown Commissioners (because of the sites inter-tidal location), the Department of Trade and Industry's off-shore and on-shore units.

Audits have been carried out for the Environment Agency as part of the routine Integrated Pollution Control. The CATS team uses these audits extensively as an internal tool to improve standards or performance, within the Total Quality culture of 'Continuous Improvement' (CI). As part of Amoco's total quality approach there is a high level of training and awareness among staff and contractors about environmental considerations.

Where necessary, contractor agreements have specified non-disturbance clauses, and briefings to personnel about SSSI requirements, so as to minimise the impact on rare species.

FUNDING AND PARTNERS

The total investment by the CATS group in all phases of the CATS terminal will amount to a total of £600 million, and many of the environmental measures that have been taken have been at no or negligible additional cost. The environmental elements of the overall design represent approximately 0.5% of total costs, but the integrated objectives make it difficult to separate environmental from other elements.

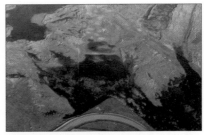

CATS environmental challenge – a site of special scientific interest

The whole CATS operation costs around £5.5 million per year to run; maintaining the reed pond will costs an estimated £4-5,000.

Protecting the wayleaves along the pipelines coastal route

Partners in the CATS group include:

AMOCO; British Gas; HESS; Phillips; FINA and AGIP.

English Nature and INCA: major advisory partners in many of the design aspects of the project. English Nature was the channel for consultations with many other bodies, such as the RSPB, with whom they were in regular contact, and were able to hold generic meetings. English Nature is not seen in a policing capacity (in relation its statutory role for the SSSI), but there to advise and enhance activity. INCA have helped this project and a number of other operations locally, with implementing standards: Amoco greatly values the presence of local industry and nature bodies.

The Cleveland Wildlife Trust: participated in the initial site survey work; their local knowledge has been invaluable to the project.

Local Authorities/Agencies: Stockton Borough Council, the Northern Development Company, Tees-side Tomorrow Ltd and Teesside Development Corporation are formally listed as partners to the CATS investment. Councillors are, in general, quite well informed about the development as a number have chemical industry backgrounds.

Teesmouth Bird Club: had taken an interest in the development, and Amoco was able to provide a bird watching hide with disabled access on the Seal Sands. This was set up very inexpensively in liaison with the site contractors, some of whom had birdwatching interests. The hide was formally launched by the Wildlife Trust.

Schools: partnership with local schools has included sponsoring a Cleveland Wildlife Trust Exhibition on industry and nature and financing coach travel to it by local schools who would not otherwise have the funds to attend; an information pack for children; some work experience, largely arranged through staff on the site; small scale visits (although it was pointed out that gas processing does not provide a great deal of visual excitement).

The CATS terminal on Seal Sands, Teeside

OUTCOMES

The team are proud of protecting existing wetland areas, orchids, foxes and wild birds. In an industry not well known for sentimentality, one member of the technical staff commented that 'it (excitement about the environmental achievements) all starts to rub off on you after a while'.

The controlled documents (required by the Integrated Pollution Control Act) are used as an audit trail tool within the company to measure performance and look at wider aspects of activity and to work towards Continuous Improvement. The Act requires a rigorous system of three yearly resubmissions, annual submissions and quarterly updates on discharges, by agreement with the Environment Agency.

The company is now working with Durham University, and there are plans for a post graduate student from the university (probably and ecology student) to undertake an extended monitoring exercise.

LESSONS FOR GOOD PRACTICE

- The widest possible, and timely consultation is essential. By talking to a wide audience early on, presenting a consistent message, and being open to ideas and advice from those being consulted, objections and problems can be tackled before they reach planning application stage. Organisations such as English Nature can often suggest ways of improving plans and involving communities that need not be costly.

- Local authority recommended consultee lists for pre-planning consultations are strongly recommended by AMOCO and English Nature. DoE should consider drawing up a format/range of questions to ensure that, as far as possible, advance planning takes place. This will often make savings of time and money, streamline the local authority planning process and improve projects by enabling good practice to be designed in at the outset.

- The CATS Team has a policy of sharing all information wherever possible. Particularly with major construction plants of this nature, anxieties normally focus on the unknown. A simple briefing document, setting out what the company is trying to do, circulated widely is generally a good investment. The company also tries to answer all correspondence from the public, which is what would be expected of a 'decent corporate citizen'.

Consultation in action – CATS, INCA and English Nature

- Consistent and enforceable arrangements with all contractors - and full explanation of the reasons for them - are important to avoid disturbance of wildlife and plants.

Contact: Richard Bond, Gas Transportation Manager, Seal Sands Road, Middlesborough, Cleveland TS2 1UB

4.3 Business Environment Association

INTRODUCTION AND KEY ISSUES

In 1991, at an early stage of its work with small businesses, Groundwork Blackburn learnt that the hardest and most expensive task facing them was convincing senior management that environmental matters are relevant to profitability. It therefore developed a range of services and organisations designed to increase efficiency, improve the business environment, reduce waste, introduce innovation and assist with new protocols or UK or EU laws and regulations.

ACTION TAKEN

A Business and Environment Association was established which now has 130 members in the Blackburn and Darwen area who pay an annual membership fee of between £25 and £450. All major employers in the area were early members, but the bulk of the members are now SMEs.

The activities of the Association include on-site consultations, seminars and newsletters. The aim of the Association is to raise awareness of green issues and how they affect business profitability, and to keep members informed of changes in environmental standards and regulations.

The increased knowledge of these issues then encourages members to use the environmental services offered by Groundwork and a number of other providers.

Through these providers practical support can be given, including detailed surveys on energy and waste problems, with recommendations on energy conservation and waste minimisation, waste disposal, discharge consents. Services provided include:

Environmental Management Service: this offers consultancy advice which looks in detail at the individual needs of businesses and which is specifically geared to their business objectives rather than 'pure' greening matters.

Environmental Resource and Information Centre (ERIC): this provides a proactive and reactive service to companies wishing to get abreast of changing standards and regulations.

Landscape Design Consultancy: a service provided to any local business or other organisation.

The Brightsite Scheme: companies are shown how creative environmental improvements can help to make premises more attractive, functional and yet cost effective to maintain.

Although these projects have been indicated under separate headings they form, in effect, a cohesive programme with companies taking advantage of several programmes.

PARTNERS AND FUNDING

The Groundwork Trust, Blackburn: one of the earliest Groundwork Trusts, it has played a pivotal role in the development and management of both the Association and the support activities provided to the business community.

Blackburn City Challenge

Blackburn Borough Council and Lancashire County Council: the two local authorities have been involved in a variety of ways, including strategic assistance and finance.

The private sector: the private sector is proving to be the most rapidly growing element of the partnership in three ways:

- by joining the Association and therefore funding core dissemination and information;
- by becoming actively involved in the environmental debate;
- by purchasing services from Groundwork, thus enabling a solid core of local, experienced staff to be established.

The Department of the Environment: the DoE is a core funder of the Groundwork Trust movement.

There is now an annual budget of approximately £450,000, made up of a complex cocktail of subscriptions, grants, and fees coming from the above partners or earned in the market place.

OUTCOMES

For the years 1990-96 the Groundwork Trust claim the following 'business' outputs for their activities:

- 130 members of the Business Environment Association;
- 160 environment reviews undertaken;
- 32 seminars held;
- 2,600 managers on environmental training courses;
- 25 companies working on BS7750/EMAS Regulation projects;
- £4.5 million on environmental works by Groundwork clients;
- 90 Brightsite sketch schemes prepared;
- £125,000+ of work implemented on Brightsite schemes;
- £850 million client turnover influenced.

Cumulatively, the project is beginning to have a much wider impact than would be apparent from looking at the individual projects.

As an example, both the Chair and Deputy Chair of the Environment Association are people whose companies were helped in the early stages of work. As leading business people themselves they are very effective communicators to the business community about environmental matters and the commercial advantages of being environmentally aware.

Some of the companies are now working with their employees on environmental schemes within the wider community, and particularly with schools.

Several of the sites which have been improved are important 'gateway' sites for the entire town and their transformation is deemed to have an important effect on encouraging inward investment and tourism. Chief amongst these is the Gilbraith Transport site, where a combination of stone cleaning and 18 new award winning murals have transformed the railway 'gateway' into the town.

As will be readily appreciated, the greening of individual sites has an effect, not only for the individual company and its employees, but also for the entire community surrounding that site.

LESSONS FOR GOOD PRACTICE

- The work of developing new contacts with SMEs will generally need public sector support because it is time consuming and not cost effective. As relationships develop, a larger pool of interested companies can lead projects like this to produce a sizeable part of their costs from the sale of services to the private sector. The business community needs development and capacity building in environmental matters as much as a community group might need capacity building for business issues.

- The Chair and Deputy Chair of the Trust are business people and 'converts' to the environmental cause. They are used extensively by the Trust to open doors at both a company and strategic level. Business people are more likely to listen to a business leader than an 'environmentalist'.

- Greening, energy efficiency and waste management are not 'add-ons' to a successful business, but items which can directly effect the profitability.

- Although this is clearly a business advisory service which is part funded by the TEC and Economic Development Unit of the local authority, there are no effective links with the Business Link. Consideration needs to be given to how this can best be achieved.

- There needs to be a greater strategic level of thinking for this project. Although it has clear linkages with the Council's other mainstream economic development activity, there is an impression that this is a stand alone item rather than part of a cohesive strategy.

Contact: Groundwork Environment Centre, Bob Watts Building
Nova Scotia Wharf, Bolton Road, Blackburn, Lancashire, BB2 3GE

5.1 Hillsborough Walled Garden, Sheffield

Walled Garden

INTRODUCTION AND KEY ISSUES

This case study illustrates how local authorities can empower communities to take local ownership of space. Hillsborough Park's walled garden 'old nursery' area is within sight and sound of Sheffield Wednesday's Football Stadium (scene of the stadium disaster): it had been in a state of dereliction after its horticultural training centre for council gardeners closed in 1987, and was facing proposals to turn it into a parking area, which was not a popular choice.

Following the Hillsborough disaster, there was an important need to provide a quiet, secluded memorial area for bereaved families, as well as green open space and an activity base for special needs groups.

ACTION TAKEN

The project's aims and objectives were established and set out as follows:

- to reclaim the Walled Garden;
- to facilitate access for the public;
- to create opportunities for people living in Sheffield to be involved in the planning, design and implementation;
- to create gardening opportunities for the public, particularly people with disabilities, and school groups;
- to recognise and create within the garden areas for:
  - wild life study and appreciation,
  - physically and visually disabled people,
  - peace and quiet,
  - a rose garden;
- to rehabilitate outbuildings as classrooms and a training area;
- to create a suitable memorial garden for the Hillsborough Disaster;
- to make provision for long term maintenance;
- to set up a working partnership between public, private and voluntary sectors;
- to maximise voluntary effort;
- to raise enough funds to ensure that the project can be implemented and sustained.

Initially a small group of parents from Hillsborough School became involved in the Hillsborough Park Working Group. They were keen to see a programme of improvement works in the Park as a whole, in part because local school playgrounds generally provided no more than tarmac. They quickly saw the potential of the Walled Garden, both as open space, and as a badly needed activity base for special needs groups.

Project Working Group Membership (in 1991) included:

City Councillors and officers, the Hillsborough and District Environmental Association, Hillsborough Community Development Trust, and Hillsborough School, bringing together others - both lay and professional - to develop and promote the project.

Advice came from BBC Gardeners' World, Civic Trust, Construction Industry Training, Friends of the Earth, Gardening for the Disabled Trust, Henry Boot Inner City Ltd, Horticultural Therapy, David Hamerton RICS, David Bellamy, Sheffield University, and others.

Consultation

Through wide consultation with local groups and individuals the Working Group concluded that the Walled Garden could help to serve the needs of physically disabled people, those with impaired vision and school groups. These were given as many opportunities as possible to take part in the planning, implementation and long term care of the project.

Walled Garden: early days

Fundraising was a major consideration. Traditionally, funding such a garden area would have been a City Council responsibility, but no funds were available. The Council, however, saw the scope to explore a more explicit partnership with the community and assigned an outreach development worker to help the project forward.

Volunteer effort was encouraged by inviting schools and other groups to adopt part of the garden. In addition, many of the required inputs and services for the garden were made or supplied locally, so local firms were invited to donate services, such as design, goods, and greenhouse glass, rather than cash - both for the project and as fundraising prizes. An article in the local press generated free help with garden and wildlife area design.

The Hillsborough Community Development Trust has its own fundraising committee, which worked closely with the Working Group to ensure, among other things, proper coordination and target setting. The Trust established a hit list of local firms and top companies (known to have an interest in funding environmental projects), with advice from the Ethical Investment Research Service Ltd.

Other potential sources of income included: sale of produce, a community gardening service, council grants, hire charges (rooms/equipment/tools), covenants and subscriptions. Volunteer fundraising included book sales, treasure hunts, competition and 'scavenging'.

OUTCOMES

The project was formally opened in April 1992, on the third anniversary of the disaster. None of the capital funding had come from central or local government. It has become a self-sustaining, community managed leisure resource, which provides for a wide audience and has a significant environmental impact on the local area.

Specific areas within the garden include: a garden specially for visually impaired people (designed by a blind student), with strong scents, bright colours and interesting textures; areas for local schools and community groups to adopt and develop as they wish; areas with raised beds for people in wheelchairs; a wildlife area for pond-dipping and study (for which local children have made bird, bat and hedgehog boxes); a classroom for environmental or other specimen study.

The Walled Garden has won the Times/BitC Community Enterprise Award for 1993 - improving the environment section, and in 1994 was successful with an ILAM Open Space Management Award.

FUNDING AND PARTNERS

The original estimated total cost of the scheme was around £115,000. However, by maximising input from volunteers (an estimated 12,000 hours by the opening date), training organisations, schools, colleges and the Probation Service, and getting many of the materials from businesses free of charge, fundraising needs were greatly reduced. Many local people also donated plants or cuttings.

The Hillsborough Development Trust (set up in 1990): wrote to over 70 trusts, foundations and companies in the hope that they would become partners: they received many provisional expressions of support. The trust then developed its funding strategy, which was to secure funding in roughly the following proportions:

Voluntary effort	30%
Contributions	20%
Local fund raising	10%
Company donations	10%
Grants from trusts	30%

Walled Garden: after local efforts

Sheffield City Council: in the absence of large scale local authority funding, the City Council's Recreation Department assigned an outreach development officer to work with the local community. The City Council approved the principle of a working partnership in which the community assumed the maintenance and day to day management responsibility for the park, but this is still being discussed. It was anticipated that subsequent financial assistance would be received from the TEC, European Funds, Community Action or similar programmes. Within the framework of its Parks Regeneration Strategy, innovative approaches such as this could be a major force in transforming the future management of public parks in the area.

Family Support Group: support came from the Hillsborough Family Support Group, based in Liverpool, to dedicate part of the garden as a memorial.

Community Service/Probation/Trainees: the services of the Probation Service and its charges were very important in keeping costs down, and as a form of crime prevention. Trainees rebuilt the walls, which were Grade II listed, and therefore needed to be rebuilt using correct materials.

The partnership approach to exploring future funding for extended activities (probably from the TEC, English Partnerships, or Europe) reflects the Council's view of the future: to empower communities to take ownership of space.

Walled Garden during construction

LESSONS FOR GOOD PRACTICE

- Planting does not *have* to be formal and subject to detailed design. Here, people simply plant things where there are gaps. This works because of the levels of gardening expertise around (the planting areas looked after by local groups are designed by the groups).

- Using probationers to help with the rebuilding work is likely to have helped its preservation: the people doing the work were proud - and protective - of what they had done.

- It was also thought to be important to research thoroughly the priorities and requirements of those being approached for contributions, and to put forward only realistic, quality applications.

- Good relations with the local press are a priority, especially the free press. In a local press article the team had asked for garden design assistance, and succeeded in getting free design services.

- Special needs can be tested in a practical way: as the work progressed, disabled people were invited to tour the garden, to make sure that access was adequate.

- Work with schools forms an important part of the continuing nurturing process: following a recent fire in the greenhouse area, thought to be a child's prank that got out of hand, action was taken early on to contact local schools and put across a positive message about caring for the garden - focusing on the people dear to the children who used the walled garden.

Contact: Jenny Lightowler, Hillsborough Community Development Trust
       Anfield House, 481 Langsett Road, Sheffield

5.2 Sowe Valley, Coventry

INTRODUCTION AND KEY ISSUES

The Sowe Valley is one of four strategic green corridors which penetrate the densely built up area of Coventry. The land is in predominantly public ownership (80%) and performs an important strategic role in supporting a range of different land uses, functions and wildlife habitats, together with sustaining high levels of human activity. Up until the mid 1980s the landscape of the Sowe Valley had suffered from an ad hoc and uncoordinated management regime. Some areas had also suffered misuse and deterioration as a result of increased recreational pressure and anti-social behaviour, while others remained inaccessible and unsafe.

Coventry City Council recognised the importance of the valley for its environmental and recreational potential and embarked upon an ambitious plan to shape the resource into a 1,000 acre, eight mile linear nature park for Coventry.

This case study provides an example of how one local authority has approached the planning, management and maintenance of a strategic area of the green belt in a positive, comprehensive and cost effective manner.

ACTION TAKEN

Strategy Development

Following the demise of the West Midlands County Council, the City Council took responsibility for its own strategic land use policy making. In relation to its green belt, the Council wished to encourage the positive use of the landscape, based on a detailed understanding of its operation.

In relation to the Sowe Valley, a 'corridor' study was begun in 1986. It was intended to provide a practical outworking of more general green belt policies and to provide the framework for implementation and management. The study was prepared by officers in the planning department, overseen by a small cross departmental working group of council officers, reflecting three of the five City Council land owning departments of the valley.

Signposting and information boards provide overall identity

A project officer from the planning department was given the responsibility for developing the strategy. His first task was to evaluate the landscape qualities and use made of each part of the valley. The valley was divided into nine sections and the project team looked at issues including:
- land use and character;
- the intensity and nature of use;
- access both by foot and car;
- circulation and accessibility by a variety of different users;
- landscape features including field boundaries and mature trees;
- the natural history;
- opportunities for introducing new planting to screen intrusive development on the fringes of the valley, for increasing accessibility and removing eyesores;
- opportunities for exploiting the recreational and educational potential;
- opportunities to encourage greater natural diversity and increase the nature conservation value;
- conflicts between uses and functions.

A draft plan was produced which categorised the various parts of the valley into:
- land for informal recreation with unrestricted public access;
- land for formal recreation;
- schools and playing fields;
- land to remain for agricultural use or allotments;
- land subject to major landscape improvement including mixed woodland planting;
- natural history sites.

The route of a long distance footpath was defined within the land use plan, identifying where existing footpaths could be used and where new footpaths, bridges, car parks and play areas would be needed.

Within this framework over 100 individual actions were identified, aimed at upgrading the landscape; improving/managing vehicular and pedestrian access; promoting informal/formal recreation; protecting and enhancing the nature conservation value; improving safety; enhancing boundary and screen planting; and improving management.

This framework plan formed the basis of a major first stage consultation exercise. Some 20,000 leaflets were sent out and residents were invited to visit displays in community centres throughout the area. Each display was staffed by officers from the local authority and responses to the plan were collated. A parallel consultation process was initiated involving partners, potential funding agents and local groups.

A section of the new long distance path

Community Involvement

Projects identified as part of the strategic plan have been progressed to implementation with the assistance of two field officers (employed under the City Council's Countryside Project, part funded by the Countryside Commission and with a remit to encourage community involvement in environmental projects) working closely with the community. In the discussions with the Council it was noted that they felt, over the course of the project's life, that they had seen their role shift from implementation to one of facilitator and enabler, with the Sowe Valley providing the strategic framework within which community action could be developed. One example of a 'local action' project has been the creation of a community woodland and a wildflower meadow near a comprehensive school. As with many of the projects, an established residents' association approached the field officer, seeking to improve the nature conservation value of a former sportsfield next to the school. The field officers assisted the community in the design of the area, implementation and its subsequent management. They also helped residents to access funds that would not have been available to the City Council. Some £5-6,000 was raised from English Nature, Shell Better Britain, and the Countryside Commission.

The implementation and subsequent maintenance of the project has been undertaken by the community, although more large scale maintenance works remain the responsibility of the Council.

Design

Key design features of the project include:
- *Identity*: signage and interpretation boards have been specifically designed and provide an overall identity and image to the Sowe Valley. This, coupled with a series of publicity leaflets, has helped shift perceptions of the valley as a collection of individual spaces serving a local population to that of a linear park for the whole city to use.
- *Maintenance*: low maintenance planting techniques have been adopted in all areas outside formal amenity areas which respond to the prevailing character and nature in an informal and natural way.
- *Management*: management plans have been drawn up for a number of more specialist areas. However, these remain unimplemented due to a lack of the necessary skills within the contracting organisation.
- *Safety*: a critical issue has been to ensure that the area feels secure and has included car park design, choice of plant materials, and thinning of woodland edges.

Implementation

The proposals in the study were implemented in two different ways: by capital spending on new projects, and by the introduction of more appropriate and targeted management regimes for recreation and the landscape.

In order to spread finance evenly and ensure a build-up of the revenue budget for the maintenance of new schemes, it was decided that the project should be carried out over a five to ten year period. The various projects were prioritised according to need and the associated benefits that would accrue. The strategy framework provided the basis for bids for capital finance.

Many of the major proposals were implemented by the City Council, either through direct labour or through MSC/Employment Training schemes. However, the abolition or changing nature of these schemes has affected the running of the project, particularly the ending of the Community Action Programme. Alternatives are being considered, including links with colleges.

In addition to the main projects, many smaller tree planting, access and fencing schemes, nature trails, community woodlands and habitat creation schemes were undertaken by volunteers from schools, local community and conservation groups in association with Coventry's Countryside Project.

FUNDING AND PARTNERS

- *Local Authority:* majority landowner, various departments participated in the preparation of the overall strategy and implementation of projects on the ground;

- *Countryside Commission:* provided funds for field officers under the Countryside Project;

- *Community:* user, means of implementation and, in many cases, manager of projects.

Finance was obtained from a variety of different sources, The City Council financed the project to the tune of £20,000 per annum for five years. Additional funds ware obtained from English Nature; the former Community Programme; Employment Training; Warwickshire Wildlife Trust; Urban Programme; The Countryside Commission; Derelict Land Grant; Forestry Commission.

The bidding criteria associated with a number of grant regimes and their short term nature have influenced the way the project has been implemented over time. Implementation has been driven by the availability of funds rather than appropriate phasing, resulting in certain works being undertaken too early, or at too fast a rate, in the process.

OUTCOME

A positive approach to the management of neglected and under-utilised land has resulted in a linear park which provides a valuable recreational and educational resource.

LESSONS FOR GOOD PRACTICE

- The adoption of low cost, naturalistic planting and colonisation techniques have produced more self-sustaining environments and as a result have reduced revenue costs.

- Low cost, naturalistic countryside landscapes can be successfully accommodated within city centres.

- Extensive community involvement has released voluntary labour, community management and maintenance, and attracted additional funds.

- Maintenance contracts need to be complemented by effective management plans and a ranger service, and in certain cases it may prove appropriate to make certain landscapes the subject of specialist competitive tenders.

- The presence of field officers charged with encouraging community involvement has facilitated a number community led projects, beyond the initial strategy framework.

- The production of an overall strategy formed the basis for funding bids to a variety of different sources.

- Single ownership, consistent political support, and the appointment of a cross department steering group have been crucial for fund allocation, project development and maintenance.

- There is market for specialist landscape contractors with the skills and equipment to undertake cost effective management of naturalised landscapes and wildlife habitats.

Contact: Andy Duncan, Senior Planning Officer, City of Coventry, Planning Department,
Tower Block, Much Park Street, Coventry, CV1 2PY.

5.3 Whitmore School, Hackney, Environmental and Recycling Initiative

INTRODUCTION AND KEY ISSUES

This is an example of a project that has been raising environmental awareness among schoolchildren and developing a range of imaginative and complementary environmental projects, which fit in with the local authority's overall environmental agenda, whilst coping with a climate of diminishing resources.

Whitmore School: hazel hurdles protect butterfly and bee areas

ACTION TAKEN

A series of inter-related initiatives have taken place: some to improve the playground area, with a small grant from Groundwork Hackney, and involving pupils in the processes; some highly opportunistic, as a result of winning competitions; and others linked to recycling initiatives, initially with Hackney Task Force funding.

Since 1992 the school had been working on environmental educational issues with the Hackney Environmental Education Project, until funding for the latter was withdrawn.

Action to develop structures

Much of the activity has been led by the Whitmore Action Group for the Environment (WAGE), set up by the school as a vehicle for broadening community involvement and fundraising. WAGE is open to everyone in the school community, although there is a small management committee including representatives of governors, staff and parents, and a sub-committee on fundraising.

Recycling and other environmental activity

The school was one of a number funded by Hackney Task Force to use bins for recycling cans, white paper and textiles. The school has also won a number of competitions, the prizes for which have included:

- the services of an 'environmentalist-in-residence' for a term, to help WAGE to get started, and to work with class teachers for example in arranging visits and planning the environmental aspects of topic work. Each class then produced from its topic work a statement for a School Charter for the Environment;

- environmental books, planters, money for recycling bins and improvements to the playground shelter.

The recycling bins earn the school a modest income, which goes towards environmental improvements in the school grounds, and recycling has now been extended, through an outside firm, to include newsprint and magazines.

The local authority's Recycling Officer also gave the school an 'indoor' compost bin, which was supplemented outside by compost containers. These provide compost from household and garden waste to produce organically grown plants and vegetables in the school grounds.

Environmental work has included painting the outside shelters, linked to topic work on 'images and perceptions' using mural designs developed with 'Freeform', a community arts organisation. Individual classes have taken responsibility for a planter where the children can grow their own plants and shrubs.

Through Environment Week 1995, and Groundwork's Greenlink project, the whole school had a link with Sainsburys to look at the company's recycling activities. This arose when the teacher saw Groundwork's newsletter, which mentioned the GreenIT and Greenlink projects, and saw the potential for linking up with the school's focus on recycling.

Tree planting, by the children and volunteers, extends to 2,000 trees (financed by the local authority). Bee and butterfly areas have been created, protected by hazel hurdles which the children helped to make, as well as living willow tunnel structures for play and quiet areas. There is an ambitious and extensive 'master plan' for improving an existing play area, and plans for an area which is at present derelict, to become a quiet area. The design was drawn up as part of a planning for real exercise carried out free by CLAWS (21 hours of free services). It will be implemented as and when funds permit - an estimated £160,000. These plans include pergolas, a maze, musical stepping stones, an extended pond area and wildflower meadow, and an organic gardening area. There are also plans, subject to funding, to work on a historical and nature mural for the school's centenary in 1997.

The developments have included:

- the establishment in 1994 of WAGE. It has applied for charitable status now, and will need to make some changes to its constitution as a result;

- Open Days, at the first of which the new local Chair of Environmental Services became persuaded of the value of the activity, and a Grounds Day to encourage awareness, and greater use of the resources by a wider range of staff (the success of these events seems to depend greatly on weather conditions on the day);

- a newsletter, known as the Little Green Magazine, which was compiled by an under twelves group from various local schools, printed by the Borough, and circulated to every class for under twelves in Hackney. This was partly to raise awareness of the issues, and to encourage other children to come up with ideas for making Hackney 'a better place for the 21st Century', and take part in activities which will 'help save our planet';

- a wildlife 'watch club' which monitors frog, bird and other activities;

- participation by the children in Blue Peter and local radio programmes, which has been a source of great excitement for many of the children;

- various events for the Whitmore Action Group for the Environment including tree planting, tree dressing and discos.

Whitmore School: children at work on the hurdles

The projects focus on indigenous trees and flora and their maintenance and management has needed careful thought. What maintenance had previously been undertaken routinely by the Council has been contracted out, but sensitive mowing is now needed to take account of areas such as the bee and butterfly areas. The Tower Hamlets Environment Trust has weeded around the trees, applied mulches, and undertaken more specialist management and tasks with local children. The aim is, gradually, to devolve some of the tasks to the children. The school is also hoping to work with Age Concern to get older people in the surrounding area to become involved in gardening with the children.

As part of overall community development, there are intentions to draw up a skills register of staff, parents and others so as to maximise the scope for involvement and use of appropriate skills.

PARTNERS

The Whitmore Action Group for the Environment: this group has led the work and provided the bulk of volunteer support to carry out tasks such as planting. It is gradually developing, and involves formal representation from pupils through their School Council. Staff and parents are also involved, and the group's acting chair is a local representative of the London Wildlife Trust;

Hackney Task Force: provided the recycling bins as part of a programme for a number of schools in whose catchment areas the Task Force Area is located;

CLAWS (designers): worked with children from the school Council on a planning for real exercise which resulted in the extended garden design;

London Borough of Hackney: eight or nine other schools are involved in similar schemes, only one of them at secondary level. Borough architects are working with several other schools, often in close cooperation with Groundwork;

The Borough Environmental Services: contributed £5,000 for tree planting, and the Borough's Parks Department £500 for a compost shredder and shrubs. Agenda 21 representatives have also been most helpful in an advisory capacity;

Groundwork Hackney: has been a source of advice on many issues often in cooperation with the local authority/education business partnership, and contributed £250 to the work on the shelter, through its small grants scheme;

BT: made an award worth £100 in Environment Week;

Thames Water and the Hackney Education Business Partnership: worked together on a water cycle mural for the school;

Education Industry (CSCS): funded the three willow structures and a den (£600);

The Ernest Cook Trust: contributed £100;

Tower Hamlets Environment Trust: have obtained the appropriate trees, and given technical advice and assisted with specific tasks such as mulching and weeding.

OUTCOMES

Areas and features previously vandalised by pupils are now used much more constructively, and play areas have been made attractive. The children are taking a much more active interest in caring for, and learning about, their environment.

LESSONS FOR GOOD PRACTICE

- Individual commitment needs to be strong. The teacher leading this work has adopted a proactive and imaginative approach, in a climate of diminishing resources, to incorporate environmental awareness into a range of learning activities, and to develop a sense of stewardship among the children. There is scope for helping other staff to exploit the potential the new and extending facilities offer for curriculum and pupil motivation.

- The Borough's broader consideration of local Agenda 21 and incorporation of environmental issues into Council thinking has had an unmistakably positive impact on shaping developments in this school and others in the area.

- There is a firm view that involving the children as much as possible gives them a sense of ownership, and of fun. Taking part in programmes such as Blue Peter has significantly increased their motivation and confidence levels.

- Much of the activity has been small scale and opportunistic, exploiting success in competitions (the winning of which is also a powerful motivator), but within the framework of an overall strategy. The phasing of activity can be managed to accommodate funding constraints: it relies on key staff keeping up to date on funding regimes and on the scope for 'bringing in free resources'. This is, however, both demanding and time consuming.

- Developing a skills register helps to maximise the scope for involving the wider community and enveloping capacity.

Contact: Ms Sandra McLeod, WAGE
Whitmore School, Bridport Place, London N1 5JN

5.4 Cramlington Organisation for Nature and Environment (CONE)

INTRODUCTION AND KEY ISSUES

Blyth Valley Council realised that, in common with many new towns, Cramlington's green spaces had little character or diversity in terms of landscape, habitat type or species. Community involvement in wildlife and environmental issues was also limited. CONE was established in 1991 as a free standing organisation to improve the environment and promote community involvement.

ACTION TAKEN

Blyth Valley Council established CONE as an independent operation from the outset, as they realised that an holistic approach to the environment would require a partnership from a variety of groupings. Secretariat and core staff were seconded from the local authority.

The project works by stimulating interest in the environment through direct approaches to the different organisations and companies within the area, and working with them, on a site by site basis, to review the potential for creating more interesting, bio-diverse areas within their land holdings. This approach is aided by a high quality progressive programme of publicity which has stimulated considerable interest in CONE's activity. CONE provides practical support and assembles partners for each project, and is the route for grant funding to supplement the financial input from the host partner. It then encourages the host organisation to expand its activities and to promote visitors to its site.

While most of the work is site by site, wildlife corridors link individual sites. The quantity of sites now being attended is of great strategic importance to the development of the town.

It works in four different ways:

- *natural habitat creation:* the creation of wildlife habitats in public spaces, schools and business grounds to promote bio-diversity, innovative land-use, low cost environmental maintenance and involvement in works of nature;

- *school nature areas:* similar to the above but with a special emphasis on the creation of wildlife areas within schools so that they can be used in a variety of ways in relation to the National Curriculum;

- *raising awareness:* provision of a series of activities designed to make residents of all ages more aware of conservation potential and issues;

- *wildlife corridors:* the creation of wildlife corridors through the town.

FUNDING AND PARTNERS

- *Blyth Valley District Council:* an important source of finance, contacts and practical support. The core staff of the project are two senior members of the planning department who devote approximately 40% of their time to this initiative;

- *Northumberland County Council:* help provide contact with schools and a considerable input from specialist education advisers;

- *Northumberland Wildlife Trust:* assistance with advice and expertise and linkages to wider strategies;

- *The private sector:* Merck Sharp & Dohme, INKEL, Knoll, Fasson - provide core funding for CONE but most also run their own habitat projects either on site or in the community, or assist with CONE projects in schools;

- *Northumbrian Water:* central funders of CONE. Specific help provided for water and wetland projects;

- *English Nature:* formerly a significant contributor of small grants for individual projects, it now largely provides advice and encouragement to the main project and its sub projects;

- *Northern Electric:* core funder of CONE and co-funder of a teacher outreach worker post working with the schools;

- *The local community:* increasingly involved in projects such as the House Martin survey, and support for schools projects;

- *Schools:* most of the schools in Cramlington now have a wildlife habitat which is supported in some way or introduced through CONE.

The total core costs of running CONE are approximately £52,000 per year which are met by the above partners.

OUTCOMES

This project is highly innovative, low cost, and is having a tremendous effect on the appearance of this still relatively new 'new' town. Its success is difficult to measure in hard outputs. Projects tend to be small but highly used. One new school habitat, for example, can create learning experiences for more than 300 children a year and continue to do so for many years.

Much of the change is in the appearance of land; underused, open grassed areas have been replaced by more diverse landscaping and planting which are giving considerable pleasure to large numbers of people.

Success for a project like this can best be measured against the number of people who wish to participate in it and the willingness to become involved if asked. Of the fifteen local schools, thirteen are involved.

Knoll Pharmaceuticals started with a small lake project but have now created a major wetland and are creating a 2 hectare wildlife meadow inside their boundary. The three projects are visited on average by three schools each week for specific activities. Previously no visits at all were made to these areas which, with the exception of the lake, were grassed. Other companies are now following their example.

Residential areas ranging from sheltered accommodation for the elderly to blocks of flats, are seeking help in establishing their own wildlife habitats.

LESSONS FOR GOOD PRACTICE

- The involvement of schools was a priority for all concerned because of the nature of the vandalism and other problems. The schools use the habitats in a number of ways. In addition to the strictly 'environmental' areas of the national curriculum they are also used for number work, art, domestic science, French lessons and history.

- Used properly the habitats can stimulate interest in the garden at home, with parents becoming interested as a result of their children's interest.

- The Council feel that the changes have produced a much better image of their borough for visitors of all types.

- Every area has large amounts of sterile, underused or unsightly land. CONE has shown how it is possible to make habitats in places which greatly improve appearance, and can save costs.

- The project has encouraged greater interaction between the business and the residential communities.

- There are implications in these activities for the control and maintenance of large areas of monotonous grassland, whether they be in parks, on roadsides, or behind company gates.

- Parks can be converted from 'just' green spaces into more interesting appealing, places, with 'rough' areas for imaginative children's play, wild flower meadows and a variety of habitats suitable for wild animals.

Contact: Planning and Development Department, Blyth Valley Borough Council
      Seaton dela Val, Northumberland, NE25 0DX

6.1 Romford Town Centre

INTRODUCTION AND KEY ISSUES

This example illustrates the range of inter-related partnership processes and consultations that have come into play in greening Romford town centre as part of its overall revitalisation.

Romford, which was almost entirely rebuilt in the 1960s, presents a challenge for greening, particularly as the town centre has no parks and very little open space and will not have any significant vacant land until the closure of the Romford Brewery which will release an 18 acre site in the town centre. Furthermore, very few funds are available for ongoing maintenance.

ACTION TAKEN

Romford's Town Centre Manager and Economic Regeneration Unit, within the London Borough of Havering, has taken a number of steps to integrate greening and environmental improvements into the Council's thinking and decision-making processes. The Council had secured a major capital receipt early in 1994 through the sale of its interest in the main shopping centre in the town. It determined to use over £2.5 million of this in environmental improvements within the town centre, as part of a wider revitalisation strategy.

Alongside this, the Council is one of the partner authorities in a successful local Groundwork London bid to Round Two of the Challenge Fund, which will make £750,000 available over five years for public art and greening activities, not as yet fully specified.

Business Planning

The Town Centre Manager (appointed in 1994 with support from Boots, Debenhams and Marks & Spencer) took the relatively unusual step of developing a ten year business plan for Romford Town Centre.

The plan, which sets out a vision, seven key objectives and a strategy for achieving them, has been fully endorsed by the Town Centre Partnership, which includes the Council, major businesses such as Save and Prosper, landowners such as Hammersons, the Police and local community groups, as well as the Gidea Park and District Civic Society.

Specific 'greening' proposals in the plan include:

Romford Market Place after environmental improvements

- reviewing the existing provision of trees, planters and green spaces in the town centre as part of an urban design analysis;

- identifying proposals for improved integration of planting into the design framework of the centre and implement accordingly;

- developing and implementing proposals for existing green spaces and the creation of new urban spaces, both within the existing fabric and in new developments.

Work began with a study of the town centre carried out by design consultants with experience in landscape architecture. The study identified opportunities for improvements which were then incorporated into a multi-phase improvements plan.

Pilot Project: improvements to Romford market place. The Market has been in operation for centuries and remains a key attraction for the town. Work began in summer 1995. Limitations on greening here were both practical and financial; it was not in stallholders' or shoppers' interests to attract birds or to have large volumes of leaves, and any greening needed to be virtually maintenance free. The solution to this was the planting of semi-mature pin oak - *quercus palustris* - (disliked by birds and producing fairly light foliage) in lined tree pits around the edge of the area. The bulk of the market place surface was cobbled.

Phase 1: parts of South Street which had been a bleak bus channel with narrow paths on one side. The pavement area is now café terraces with semi mature pin oak and *Fraxinus Westhof Glorie* tree planting, and hanging baskets. This has been combined with traffic reorganisation.

These two phases formed the core part of an ambitious, multi-year £7.6million programme. There will be a series of smaller scale environmental and promotional initiatives, and the feasibility of introducing a light rapid transit system is also being assessed.

There will, in addition, be an urban design led development framework, to include the 18 acre Romford Brewery site, which will set out guidance and standards, including co-ordinated landscaping. The brewery site redevelopment will specify an open space.

The Unitary Development Plan (UDP), adopted in 1993, has been overtaken by events such as the brewery closure announcement and the Business Plan. The UDP seeks to minimise the use of cars and develop other transport systems.

Romford Market Place showing new tree planting

Strategic Context

The Business Plan proposes a vision that 'Romford should be at the forefront of town centres in meeting the existing and future needs of the whole community, through positive action to build on its unique strengths and qualities'.

The greening and environmental measures fall mainly under the Business Plan's sixth objective, that the town centre, 'should build on the strengths of its historic qualities and character, street pattern and structure through investment to create a high quality, well maintained environment with a distinctive and memorable identity that attracts and welcomes visitors'.

The six related strategic objectives may be summarised as follows:

- that local residents and employees regard Romford as their first choice for everyday shopping and that people in the wider region see Romford as an attractive area for shopping, so that retailers regard it as East London's principal town centre retail location;

- provision of a range of 'quality attractions' (business and employment opportunities, services, leisure, entertainment and residential) to serve the needs of local people and to attract visitors during the day or evening;

- accessibility by public, private transport (including bicycle) and on foot;

- a pedestrian friendly environment that ensures easy vehicle use and movement;

- a safe and secure location;

- a partnership approach to achieving the vision, involving all business, organisations and interest groups.

Tree species selected for Romford Market Place are disliked by birds and produce light foliage

Improvements to the environment are closely linked to elements of access and transport policy (with implications for air quality), leisure and other interdependent strands.

Local Involvement

Local involvement is a key stated strategic priority, and the local authority continues to undertake extensive consultation on its greening and related activities. Early consultees included London Regional Transport (in relation to bus routes and the light rapid transport system), Railtrack; the Police (including the positioning of trees in relation to CCTV systems); all local businesses; everyone living in the surrounding streets; the Borough's Disablement Access Officer and the local civic society. There are plans to involve local schools, through the design consultants, to develop further public art.

OUTCOMES

Work on Phase Two is in progress but the ten year plan has not yet been adopted as Council policy. However, mechanisms and procedures have been developed for effective consultation, and the framework is endorsed by key partners.

FUNDING AND PARTNERS

Greening funding issues are difficult to disentangle from the broader town centre development. Groundwork London's Challenge Fund bid brings Romford a total of £750,000 over five years.

Costs for the tree planting are estimated at a total of £218,000 for the market square, and landscape design specifications are integrated into the town centre programme. Funding for these two stages of the Environmental Improvements Programme came from the sale of the Council's interest in the 'Liberty' Shopping Centre to Hammersons and Standard Life. £2.5million has been made available for improvements in total, and further funding will be sought from other sources such as the Challenge Fund and the private sector.

The Town Centre Partnership brings together leading businesses, voluntary and trade organisations, transport operators, property owners, Havering Council and others with an interest in the town centre, to work together to achieve the vision and objectives.

Pin Oaks in Romford Market Place

LESSONS FOR GOOD PRACTICE

- Overall progress is easier when people and organisations are consulted early on, particularly over issues that are likely to be controversial. It pays to draw up lists and procedures for consultation, ensuring that the process is well documented, for future reference.

- The positioning of trees and planters needs careful thought to avoid obscuring CCTV cameras.

- Greening is not, in itself enough to bring about revitalisation: it must be part of a far wider strategy to address issues beyond greening.

- Design consultants need unambiguous briefs and active monitoring. They can be a useful resource in helping to present the arguments clearly to committees for example using photo montages or artist's impressions. Romford's progress meetings with the consultants involve the Council's designer, transport planners, legal representatives and the market place managers.

- Having design consultants who have the breadth of experience to include greening species and maintenance advice has helped to integrate these issues into the broader context. Constraints on revenue funding will, however, place some limitations on what they can recommend.

- Project management expertise on the part of design consultants is an advantage in taking the project from concept to conclusion.

CONTACT: Simon Quinn/Peter Davis, London Borough of Havering
Directorate of Environment and Planning
Mercury House, Mercury Gardens, Romford, Essex RM1 3SL

Annex 2 Members of the Advisory Group

Professor Graham Ashworth / Ms Jo Sutton, Going for Green

Mr George Barker / Ms Sue Collins, English Nature

Mr Roger Clarke, Countryside Commission

Mr John Davidson, Groundwork Foundation

Mr John Early, AMEC Developments Ltd

Mr Jed Griffiths, RTPI

Mr Tony Hams, LGMB

Dr Stewart Harding, National Heritage Memorial Fund

Mr John Lacey, Black Country Development Corporation

Professor David Lock, DoE Chief Planning Adviser

Mr Jon Rouse, English Partnerships

Mr Alan Smith, ILAM

Mr Phil Swann, AMA

Mr Alan Tate, Landscape Institute

Annex 3 The Seminar Programme

Seminar 1: Transport Corridors

Tuesday 19 March 1996: Room A (P1/012)/Room D (P1/140)
Department of the Environment
2 Marsham Street, London SW1P 3EB

Speakers: Mark Loxton, The Adams Loxton Partnership
Philip Russell-Vick, Chris Blandford & Associates

Seminar 2: Residential Areas

Thursday 21 March 1996: Room H (P3/156A)/Room C (P1/077A)
Department of the Environment
2 Marsham Street, London SW1P 3EB

Speakers: Chris Baines, Environmental adviser, writer and broadcaster
Sarah Reynolds, The Landscape Partnership

Seminar 3: Open Spaces

Wednesday 27 March 1996: Room G (P2/047)/Room M (P3/136)
Department of the Environment
2 Marsham Street, London SW1P 3EB

Speakers: Judy Walker, National Urban Forestry Unit
Rob Pearson, Sheffield Development Corporation

Seminar 4: Derelict Land

Thursday 28 March 1996: Room A (P1/012)/Room C (P1/077A)
Department of the Environment
2 Marsham Street, London SW1P 3EB

Speakers: Stephen Lee-Bapty, Planning Directorate, Department of the Environment
Robert Higham, Black Country Development Corporation

Seminar 5: Town Centres

Tuesday 16 April 1996: Room A (P1/012)/Room C (P1/077A)
Department of the Environment
2 Marsham Street, London SW1P 3EB

Speakers: Tony Rifkin, Civic Trust

Seminar 6: Industrial Land

Thursday 18 April 1996: Government Office for the North West
Sunley Tower, Piccadilly Plaza
Manchester M1 4BE

Speakers: John Lacey, Black Country Development Corporation
Ian Jeavons, Dudley Metropolitan Borough Council
Geoff Barber, English Nature

Annex 4 Select Bibliography

Aldous, T., *Inner City Urban Regeneration and Good Design* (HMSO, 1988)

Audit Commission, *Competitive Management of Parks and Green Spaces* (HMSO, 1988)

Baines, C., *The Wild Side of Town* (BBC, 1986)

Blowers, T., *Planning for a Sustainable Environment* (TCPA, 1993)

Commission of the European Communities, *Green Paper on the Urban Environment* (EU, 1990)

Davidson, J., MacEwan, A., *The Livable City* (RIBA, 1983)

Davidson, J., *How Green is Your City?* (Bedford Square Press, 1988)

DoE, *Quality in Town and Country* (HMSO, 1994)

DoE, *Involving Communities in Urban and Rural Regeneration* (HMSO, 1995)

DoE, *People, Parks and Cities* (HMSO, 1996)

DoE, *Sustainable Development: the UK Strategy* (HMSO, 1994)

Elkin, T. and McLaren, D., *Reviving the City: towards sustainable urban development* (Friends of the Earth, 1991)

Fordham, G., *Made to Last: Creating Sustainable Neighbourhood and Estate Regeneration* (JRF, 1995)

Holmes, A., *Limbering Up: Community Empowering on Peripheral Estates* (RIPE, 1992)

Llewellyn-Davies, *Open Space Planning in London* (LPAC, 1992)

Local Government Management Board, *A Framework for Local Sustainability* (LGMB, 1993)

Local Government Management Board, *Local Government for Sustainable Development* (LGMB, 1992)

Mayhew, P., *et. al.*, *British Crime Survey 1992* (HMSO, 1993)

OECD, *Environmental Policies for Cities in the 1990s* (OECD, 1990)

Tibbalds, F., *Making People Friendly Towns: Improving the Public Environment in Towns and Cities* (Longmans, 1992)

Printed in the United Kingdom for The Stationery Office
Dd 303107 11/96 C20 59226